The Memoir Writing Workbook

Memories into Memoir

A Creative Writing Journey

Irene Graham

The Memoir Writing Workbook

Memories into Memoir

Author: Irene Graham

First published in Ireland in 2009 by Irene Graham. This edition published 2018.

Kinvara, Co. Galway, Ireland

Websites:

TheMemoirWritingClub.com

TheCreativeWritersWorkshop.com

ISBN 978 0 9561811 1 4

A CIP catalogue record for this book is available from the British Library.

Printed and bound in Ireland by Print Bureau, Dublin

Design & Layout by Niall Kiernan

Note: Throughout the workbook, where the pronouns he or she are used, the non-binary pronoun, they, can be applied.

Cover Photo: Copyright © Irene Graham 1994

THE MEMOIR WRITING WORKBOOK
Memories into Memoir

Irene Graham is a writer, story editor and photographer with a background in educational studies, writing, film production and photography. In 1991 she founded The Creative Writer's Workshop, which has become an international success in fiction and memoir writing. Her online memoir writing course and private writing classes in The Memoir Writing Club provides in-depth tutoring on memoir writing to new, emerging and advanced writers. Irene's writing techniques are based upon right-brain/left-brain learning exercises that evoke recall and enhance creativity. Irene lives in the West of Ireland, writing, taking photographs and gardening – when she is not tutoring workshops!

To my wonderful family
– present, past and future

Acknowledgements

The Memoir Writing Workbook would never have come to fruition without the participation of the many enthusiastic and talented writers who traversed the globe and attended my workshops.

I am even more honoured that so many of these writers participated in a second and even third workshop. You invested your faith in me to guide you through the creative process of writing, and in so doing each and every one of you contributed to my own creative growth. For this I am eternally grateful.

Since the first publication of *The Memoir Writing Workbook* in 2009 I have been lucky to share my work in my Online Memoir Writing Course with a wider audience. It never ceases to amaze me the stories of the lives lived and the memories shared.

Thank you all, too many to mention, for your honesty, creativity and willingness to share your stories with me.

I am blessed and deeply grateful to have so many wonderful and supportive people in my life. This thank you list merely reflects a small portion of treasured friendships: Hugh Kirwan for his heart of gold, sound advice and continued support in all I do. All my technical teams over the years, especially Billy Brady and Niall Kiernan. My editor, Adrienne Murphy, for her incredible eye and attention to detail, who kept me on track and held my vision clear. Thanks to Frank Murphy and Eileen O'Gorman, talented lawyers that always steer me in the right direction.

I thank as well the friends who have inspired me and believed in me. You've made me laugh and looked out for me for a very long time. To Ciara Cronin for her continuous friendship and laughs throughout the decades. A special thanks to Linda Parker for accepting me into her lovable family. Kevin White-Barth for not only her endearing ways and ever thoughtful gestures, but for always being there. Fiona Belton for our adventures together. Janaki Welch for sharing so much. And Treasa Joyce for being the Bean an Tí of the year, every year!

This book and work would not be complete without acknowledging the late Fred Haines, fondly known to me as my adopted dad. Fred was an Oscar-nominated writer for the screenplay of *Ulysses*, a photographer, film and theatre director – but most of all, he was a wise and wonderful man who greatly inspired and influenced my life. Across continents, Fred and I communicated with each other several times a week by letter and email for 20 of the 30 years we knew one another. Sadly he passed on from this life before I completed the first draft of this workbook. Thank you, Fred, for all the guidance, words and life stories we shared together. I miss you; I miss writing to you. Thanks for the many great memories of our lives together.

CONTENTS

Introduction

Planning Your Journey – Part 3 Section 2: People

Planning Your Journey – Part 3 Section 3: Environment

Planning Your Journey – Part 3 Section 4: Structure

Introduction

As a young child I was very aware of my creativity. My formative school days were filled with colour and gaiety as I learnt and absorbed every detail of life. When I went to secondary school my world instantly grew dark and dismal. It was like entering tall dark doors of a deep cave, and I suffocated. The spontaneity of learning vanished, the ethos changed, everything became serious, and I in turn became very unhappy.

For many years I wondered what had happened in my educational process. How had I one day loved learning and felt creative and then rejected it so deeply in the second phase of my school life? It was not until I reached the age of 30 and got the opportunity to spend time on the West Coast of America that I discovered the answer – and my world of creativity blossomed again.

While studying writing at the extension programme of UCLA in Los Angeles, I researched complementary methods of education. The Bodhi Tree bookstore in West Hollywood became my second home. I sat for hours in that wonderful place and read every book in sight on education, consciousness and self-development, buying as many of them as I could afford. I researched and read night and day, joined workshops, went to lectures, spent time at model schools using complementary educational methods, and studied psychosynthesis in education with a group in Pasadena. My ability to create was reborn; my inner world was content and happy.

When I discovered right-brain/left-brain learning techniques I understood what had happened in my own education, and how and why my creativity had disappeared.

I was particularly captivated by the work of the renowned American psychologist Howard Gardner, whose work includes the theory of multiple intelligences and the uniqueness of cognitive learning. It was primarily from studying Howard Gardner's work and watching his beliefs in action in a model school in Northern California, that I understood how to integrate his theories into education – which stimulate cognitive and creative abilities.

Upon returning to Ireland in 1991, I decided that as a personal thesis, I would communicate what I'd learned during this period of my life – using creative writing as my model. Six months later The Creative Writer's Workshop was born. The workshop has evolved, expanded and grown organically over the past twenty-seven years. Throughout this time it has inspired a multitude of people from all over the globe to get in touch with their creativity through writing fiction, memoir, and autobiographical fiction.

I decided to create *The Memoir Writing Workbook* for a number of reasons. I wanted to share, on a broader scale, the sheer joy of writing. I wanted to provide an understanding of what writing memoir is about, so people could write and document their life stories for future generations. I also wanted to offer an outlet to those who feel inhibited about sharing the secrets of their lives, so that they have an opportunity to heal life wounds in private.

Since the first publication of *The Memoir Writing Workbook* in 2009, I am honoured that the workbook has helped so many to write their memoirs. It has allowed them to dig deep into their life experiences, and to show them how to turn the many incidents of their lives into story. The creation of the Online Memoir Writing Course in The Memoir Writing Club has allowed writers to gain access to tutoring, and has brought together a lively community of writers from all over the globe.

In our fast paced and ever-changing world, I feel it is almost a social responsibility now to leave at least a little of our lives in print, so that future generations will have a record of their lineage. So many stories are lost from previous generations. How many of us say 'I wish I had asked them that question, I wish they would have left us their stories, I wish I knew what their lives were like'!

Each of our stories are precious. They are the backbone of who we are, where we came from, and how we got here. And in an age of great technological change, perhaps print, and books, will be our only record of generational stories. Relying on computers and technology updates, hoping that our stories will be accessible in fifty and even a hundred years from now, may not be sufficient. And so, the argument for print remains strong. Therefore, I encourage my students not only to write their stories, but to print them as well. What could be a more precious gift?

May this workbook ignite a spark within your *yellow brick road* and may it encourage you to travel your journey using honesty and truth as your signposts. May your destination be one of deep creativity and enlightenment. And may your families remember you forever.

Now it's over to you. *The Memoir Writing Workbook* is your writing map – your guide and book of writing tools to have fun with. Go Write!

Irene G.

Ireland
2018

PART I
Rules of The Road

3

The Road to Memoir

We write to taste life twice

– in the moment, and in retrospection.

Anais Nin

Our lives are full of memories. A multitude of experiences that have shaped the paths that led us to where we are now in our personal life journeys.

Within the trillion incidents that have created our selves, what is extraordinary is that our experiences - however shared at the same moment in time with another - are nevertheless completely individual. It is this individuality and how we relate to our shared experiences that make our memories personal, our struggles interesting, and our lives unique. It is our challenge as writers to find our unique writing voice and in turn find our creative expression so that we can translate our stories into a form that will be of interest to readers.

Writing is a form of self-discovery. Through writing one gains a sense of self and healing. Writing demands reflection, and the more willing you are to be truthful with your self and examine the incidents in your life, the more intriguing your memoir becomes.

In this age of high-end technology and fast-paced living, what I refer to as 'the old world' is fast becoming extinct. The lives of our children are very different to that of our elders. It is the stories of our elders that are being lost. These stories are treasures, precious insights into life that should be written for your family and future generations – before they are buried forever.

Up until quite recently, many people believed that to be qualified to write, one had to study the classics and have a PhD in literature. The memoir genre has changed that. There is currently a great interest in personal writing; it's viewed as an art form that can be practised by anyone.

Memoir writing is not solely for the purpose of being published. Besides the desire to leave memoirs for family and friends, memoir writing is now often undertaken as a therapeutic form of medicine. It is seen as a positive method for alleviating trauma and loss, for healing life wounds. Writing is very constructive in aiding self-healing and personal development. Of course, this doesn't mean that memoir should be filled solely with the traumatic events of a life – far from it. Avoiding slipping into what has been labelled the 'misery memoir' is something we should be aware of.

As children we are inherently creative. We use our senses, we explore the world with fresh and inquisitive eyes, and our imaginations have no boundaries. As life demands more from us and as we enter the workforce and concentrate upon jobs that we don't always enjoy but *have* to do, we seem to lose our sense of exploration and become pigeon-holed and blinkered. In many circumstances, we forget to nurture our creativity, putting aside our imaginations. We lose sight of who we once were and how we feel. Our inherent creative abilities become dormant and we forget how to create. *The Memoir Writing Workbook* redresses this imbalance, showing you how to rekindle your creativity and write from the heart.

The Memoir Writing Workbook is about evoking your ability to express your truth through writing – using personal experiences as your bedrock material. It is based upon right-brain/left-brain exercises that show you ways to access your well of memory. You build upon your memoir in easy stages and engage in simple and fun exercises. On completion of the workbook, you will understand how to tap into your life experiences and know how to continue with your writing. The exercises can be used on an ongoing basis to aid creativity, imagination and creative writing.

The more you write, the more you will want to write. It is important to follow the exercises here in chronological order, one after the other. They are set out in a way that allows you to build from the foundation, step by step, as in any building project. As you progress through the workbook you will notice your writing voice change and develop. Your thoughts become focused. Your ability to create increases and your memories become refined. You will find the way – your way – of saying what you want to say, as you learn how to express yourself creatively.

Complete the workbook with personal honesty – that is the key to good memoir writing. You can decide when you complete the workbook what you want to do with your writing; you don't have to decide that before you begin. Just write and see what happens. See what comes up for you, see what the workbook helps you to let go of. See where it brings you to.

The most important thing is to have fun! Release yourself from expectation; it is your private journey, you need never show it to anyone if you choose not to but I do hope you will. My hope is that you will be inspired, that you'll read your work aloud and feel proud of what you've written.

Whatever happens to your writing when you have completed this workbook will be a bonus; least of all, you will have uncovered your life story and learnt how to write your memoir. Maybe you will give it to your family and friends. You may find a publisher that wants to publish your work. Or you may self-publish. But most of all you will have put *your* story down on paper in your unique way. You will have found something within that you were searching for when you started to write.

How to use *The Memoir Writing Workbook:*

The workbook comprises four parts, with Part 3 divided into four sections.

Part 1

- **Rules of The Road:**

– explains the ground rules for the exercises

Part 2

- **Finding Your Way:**

– outlines the elements of memoir writing and commences your journey in writing creatively

Part 3

- **Planning Your Journey:**

  Section 1: Events

– explores how to recall and map events that were significant in your life

  Section 2: People

– shows how to remember and incorporate details of people that were important to you

  Section 3: Environment

– describes how to creatively include environment and atmosphere in your memoir

  Section 4: Structure

– clarifies the necessity for structure and how to obtain it

Part 4

- **Navigating With Confidence:**

– demonstrates how to move forward with your life story and how to complete your memoir

Note: Part 3 includes many exercises that require thought and reflection. Do not be in a hurry to complete them in one sitting. Take your time, mull over the questions, and recall your answers in detail.

So get started…enjoy the adventure, be honest and write from your heart.

Packing for The Journey

Exercise I

You are about to embark upon a writing journey. You therefore need to pack!

To complete your writing journey you will need:

- *The Memoir Writing Workbook*
- a box of coloured chalk
- a box of crayons
- two A4 or letter-sized sketch pads (plain paper)
- non-lyrical music
- a pen you enjoy writing with

Learning to Navigate

The Well of Memory

Our task as memoir writers is to embrace our well of memory to find the stories that affected our path in life. These paths were influenced not only by our personal decisions but by the communities we belonged to.

Stored within each of us are our memories – what I refer to as the 'well of memory' – that collection of experiences made up of people and events in a given society that shaped our lives. We are seeking to sort those life incidents that had a particularly great impact upon us, and the decisions we did or did not make. Those significant moments that changed our present and altered our future. In reflecting upon our past we can see patterns in our history that, once ordered, can become the focus of our memoir.

As you progress through this workbook you will discover the subject and theme of your memoir. You will engage in exercises that enhance your memories and develop your life stories in easy stages. You will connect to your writing voice and the core of your life journey as you learn how to creatively express your life story through memoir.

Each exercise in the workbook has been created to help you evoke your well of memory and recall details from your past.

Your *well of memory* provides the source material for your memoir.

You will engage in many right-brain exercises that will enhance your writing while developing and strengthening your writing voice. There are no correct answers to any of the exercises. It is important that you try them all. In time you will come to notice which exercises stimulate your creativity and enhance your work.

Some of the exercises you may like, some you may find more difficult. That's OK. You may find that your writing flows more easily with some of the exercises than with others. This is normal, and happens because some exercises will appeal to your particular way of thinking, to your individual brain. It is therefore useful to put more effort into the exercises that you find more difficult. These challenging exercises will not only strengthen your thinking patterns but will also enliven your writing.

There are no rules when you write creatively, but there are some guidelines that will enhance what you have to say as you progress through the workbook.

Note: To make your journey easier and maximise your ability to navigate, it is very important to complete the exercises in the order in which they are presented in the workbook. The exercises are structured so that you will find it easy to complete your memoir and have fun while doing it. If you leave exercises out or do them in a different order you will find it more difficult to tap into your well of memory, nourish your creativity and complete the memoir you are seeking to write.

Right-Brain Tip!

Spelling: Forget about spelling correctly as you write. Spelling is of course important, as are grammar and punctuation, but what is more important at this stage is your freedom to write creatively. Spelling, grammar and punctuation are functions of editing and are controlled primarily by the left brain. When you are in a flow of writing and you stop to correct a spelling you automatically inhibit your creative flow. It is more constructive to forget about editing your work as you write, to stay in your right brain and continue to write creatively.

At a later stage you can reread your work and edit it at the same time. Then you can use your left brain, which will enable you to focus purely on editing your work.

Right! Left! Left! Right! Right! Left!

Brain Hemispheres

We need to use and work with both the left and right sides of our brains in order to develop and perform to our optimum.

Knowledge of right-brain and left-brain thinking has become more widespread throughout our society and is increasingly included in our educational systems.

The understanding of how our brains work is relatively new. Little was known about right-brain thinking abilities until World War II, when neuroscientists studied patients with brain damage. In 1981, Roger Sperry, at the California Institute of Technology, was awarded a Nobel Prize for his discoveries concerning the functional specialisation of the cerebral hemispheres. This work allowed greater insights into the specialisation of the two hemispheres of the brain.

While this workbook is not about neuroscience or how the brain works, it is important to understand a little about how we think so that you are aware of the workings of your own brain, and how you as an individual can develop it.

First, it is important to realise that it is not an advantage to be either right-brained or left-brained. We have two hemispheres in our brain – the right hemisphere and the left hemisphere – and we need to utilise both of them for optimum productivity and performance, consciously working with our strengths and developing our weaknesses.

15

Participants come to my workshops saying, "Oh, I am very right-brained," meaning they are very creative, while others say apologetically, "I only seem to function with my left brain," meaning they feel they haven't an ounce of creativity in their soul.

Neither of these views is correct. We function, whether we are aware of it or not, with both sides of our brains. We may be more developed in one side than the other, but that is our challenge. We need to develop our skills so that we can work with both sides of our brains and ultimately be able to flip from one side to the other, and perform to our optimum.

Writing certainly requires the discipline of being able to flip from one side of the brain to the other. The left side of the brain asks the questions: What do my characters look like? How will I structure my story? What is going to happen next in my story? How will I resolve the plot? It is the right side of the brain that answers these questions creatively.

Take music as an example. Most of us just hear the melody of a song – with our right brains – but the composer uses his or her left brain to arrange the notes, make the music work and integrate the music with the words. The composer is therefore using both sides of his or her brain, and this is similar to the way writers work.

- **The left side of the brain controls the right side of the body.**
- **The right side of the brain controls the left side of the body.**

Therefore, what we do with our left hand, left leg and left foot is receiving signals from the right side of the brain, and vice versa.

- **The left side of the brain is associated with analytical, linear, sequential thought.**

The left side of the brain is good at mathematics and logical thinking. It thinks sequentially and will solve a problem one step at a time. If the left brain sees a pattern, it will dissect it into parts, count the parts and even give the parts numbers.

- **The right side of the brain is associated with spatial, integrative, simultaneous thought.**

The right side of the brain is good at mental imagery and lateral and spatial thinking. It thinks in a simultaneous mode. It will look at the design of a pattern, the colours, and see how it all fits together as a whole. It will see symbols, not numbers. The right side of the brain does not count things. It sees patterns and colours.

- **The left side of the brain governs objective, precise language.**

The left side of the brain is good at reports and information; it is accurate with language and constructs words that have a precise meaning.

- **The right side of the brain governs evocative, associative and connotative language.**

The right side of the brain stores our dreamy, evocative language; it is good at making mental connections between ideas and implying additional meanings and suggestions to that of the literal meaning. It involves emotions and sensory details.

Dancing at The Crossroads
Memoir vs Autobiography

You can have many memoirs – but you (generally)

only have one autobiography.

Autobiographical writing encompasses a whole life – a life story usually written chronologically from birth to a given point in time. Thus autobiographical writing includes perhaps hundreds of characters, places and events from the writer's entire life.

Memoir writing is about drawing upon life stories and memories and focusing them into a memoir – usually upon a particular subject and the impact it had on the writer's life, eg:

- a war veteran and how he or she survived during and after a war
- a story of adoption and the search for birth parents
- the struggle through a particular illness and how it altered and changed a life
- growing up with hippy parents, living life on the road
- living in a small community in a minority race and the effect this had on adult life
- generations of a family living in one particular house and the transitions brought about over time
- the impact of the death of a child on family life
- the adventures of a woman travelling alone around the world

- a sailor's account of his or her single-handed voyage around the world
- the influence of one person upon an entire family

Memoir writing has in the recent past become a genre in its own right. It is now considered creative non-fiction, and is a popular genre in bestseller lists. In contrast to autobiographical writing in years gone by, a writer does not need to be famous or well known to write a memoir.

In our society, in which we are now more open to telling the truth of our lives, we are also more receptive to listening, sharing and learning from each other's stories. Perhaps this is the real gift of memoir – that sharing our own story we can help another to overcome similar challenges.

From my experiences of tutoring both memoir and fiction writing workshops, I find that when a writer gets in touch with their past through writing memoir, they seem to be able to transcend many of the tragic and heartbreaking events of their lives. It is as if revisiting those times through writing, being able to focus on them and learning how to put a theme and structure around them, somehow helps to wash away the pain. Memoir writing seems to allow us to keep the memories without the pain. Remarkably, what also happens when we write memoir is that we tend to remember many happy events from our lives that have somehow been buried in the sadness.

Many of my workshop participants want to write their life stories for family and friends. Some want to publish their memoirs, and others just want to complete their memoirs for themselves. For many participants, memoir writing brings them over a creative threshold and gives them a vision of what is possible. Often a curiosity develops that compels writers to embark upon fiction – using their life experiences as their base material.

Whatever has brought you to memoir writing, I urge you to continue. There is no doubt that memoir writing is a wonderful form of self-expression. Not only does it bring you to deeper places along the writing journey, but it is also cathartic, and may catapult you forward in your personal development.

When you complete this workbook, I have no doubt that something will have changed for you. You will understand more of your self, your past, your feelings and your life from here.

Checking Your Compass I

Evoking Your Senses: Sensory Thinking

Sensory learning is a powerful way for the mind to integrate

thoughts and evoke memories.

As children we used our senses automatically. We explored the world with them, letting our minds freely integrate sensory clues and signals. As adults we somehow forget to use our senses. We forget to smell the flowers, so to speak, and we rely mainly upon our sense of sight. The visually impaired do not require this sense to live a complete life, and through their ability to touch, smell, hear and taste they use these other sensory clues to determine reality.

In writing, sensory triggers are very powerful in allowing us to get in touch with feelings, emotions and memories. Sensory exercises are fun; they can lead us to all sorts of places in our writing, real and imagined, and allow us to unblock images that are stored deep within us. Sensory exercises help us to create and allow us easy access to our imaginations.

The more you explore your writing using sensory exercises, the deeper your writing and memories will become, and the freer your imagination will be. You will explore sensory learning throughout this workbook.

Sensory Exercise Tips!

Olfactory and Tactile Exercises

When you start doing sensory exercises it is much more powerful to get someone to select the object for the exercise, particularly when it is something for you to smell or touch. This allows for a surprise element in the exercise, because your brain will not know in advance what you are sniffing or touching.

Gustatory Exercise

When the sensory exercises involve taste, it is important for you to select a food item that is suitable for your personal diet. Try to find a food item that will make your taste buds tingle, like a sherbet sweet or something really sour.

Visual Exercise

Choose a family photograph or a photograph that has a lot of meaning to you, perhaps a photograph you have not looked at for a long time. Be imaginative in your visual choices.

Auditory Exercise

If you are selecting your own music to listen to in the auditory exercises, choose a piece that evokes feelings or memories, whether happy or sad. Really listen to the words and notice what images and feelings they evoke for you.

Right-Brain Tip!

The left side of your brain will want to label the scent you are sniffing or instantly name what it is you are touching.

The right side of your brain will engage with the *feeling* element of the scent or touch and what it evokes within you.

In all sensory exercises the object of the exercise is to stay with your *feelings*. Do not try to label the object or give it a name – that is the left side of your brain being analytical. Stay with your *feelings* and what the exercise evokes within you. In this way you are working with your right brain.

Connecting to Your Path I

Free Drawing

There are many times in life when we want to say something but find it difficult to express ourselves. Sometimes we don't even know what it is we want to say. There will be many moments in your writing life when you feel this way, and that's OK. It is at those times that you must look at other ways of expressing your thoughts – even the many thoughts you are not aware you want to express. Free drawing is a right-brain technique that will help.

Words are not the only way to express yourself!

Throughout the workbook you will embark upon many simple and fun drawing exercises. This is not an art class, and you will not be taught how to draw. There is no right or wrong way to express yourself with free drawing.

Note 1: Use one of the sketch pads you packed for the journey to do the drawing exercises. This will allow you to keep a record of your drawings, in sequence and all in one place.

Note 2: It is important that you use only chalk and/or crayons for these exercises. It is difficult to be precise with chalk or crayon – that is part of the purpose of the exercise.

Right-Brain Tip!

Free drawing helps to connect the right brain and the left brain. It allows the rational left brain to associate with the irrational thoughts of the right brain, making links and associating ideas. These links provide insights into memories and draw upon long-forgotten thoughts. The drawings are fun to do and allow you to think without using words.

Focal Point

Time for Me

Choose a time of the day or week to write – morning, afternoon, evening, weekend – whatever works best for you. Make a date with yourself to write.

I always tell participants in my workshops, when we talk about the discipline of writing – find whatever works for you! Find the time that works for you, make an appointment with yourself, and stick to it.

If you made a business appointment or an arrangement to meet someone, you wouldn't let them down, so don't let yourself down either. Stick to your personal appointment, and meet it consistently. There is something about doing the same thing at the same time every day or every week that our systems and brains seem to enjoy. Routine, especially a routine that gives us pleasure, is good for the soul. Try it and see if it works for you. You will feel great and that time will become so important to you that you will find yourself saying, "I can't do this or that then, that is my time to write."

If your environment is important to you, choose a special spot to write in. Make that spot yours, make it unique, so that you immediately feel comfortable when you sit down to write.

A Writing Tip!

Use the piece of non-lyrical music you packed for your writing journey in Exercise 1 to play in the background when you write. Make sure the music is calming and relaxing, perhaps music that includes flutes – something non-invasive and enjoyable, so that you almost don't notice it playing. This will help you focus your thoughts and eliminate any other distractions as you concentrate on your writing.

PART 2
Finding Your Way

Connecting to Your Path 2

Free Drawing   Exercise 2

Draw what you are feeling right now.

Use only chalk or crayons, not pens or pencils.

Depict your *feelings* through symbols and patterns. For example:

- If you are in love, this could be symbolised by drawing a heart.

- If you are angry, you might draw large teeth on the page.

- If you are sad, this could be represented by tears.

Title and date your work.

Right-Brain Tip!

The right brain sees colours, symbols and patterns. Try to use symbols and patterns to express your *feelings*.

Signposts

The Bubble Technique

Exercise 3

Visual thinking is associated with our right brain. It encompasses ways of expressing ourselves other than through words, sentences and paragraphs. Cartooning, visualisation, maps, graphs, charts, mandalas and drawing are all methods associated with visual thinking.

Used a lot in the commercial world, brainstorming and mind-mapping techniques are very effective ways to organise one's thoughts and to plan, analyse etc. When I first discovered brainstorming I was fascinated by how something so simple could help my brain to work in a different way. Through practice, I discovered how to make brainstorming work creatively in story writing, and no matter what age group I show this technique to, it works. I call it The Bubble Technique, because as with cartoons, the thoughts that are silent in your head are expressed through cartoon bubbles on the page.

The Bubble Technique is a very effective way to get through the cobwebs that seem to encase our creativity and keep us from delving deeper into what we really want to say. It allows you to get your multi-layered thoughts down on paper very quickly, so that you can define very easily what it is you really want to write and develop further.

Because thoughts and information flow through our brains so fast, it is sometimes really difficult to grasp concepts and put our ideas down on paper quickly enough. This is where The Bubble Technique helps. It eliminates the rubbish from the real and guides your brain to where it really wants to go in the development of your story.

The Bubble Technique:
- **provides access to your subconscious thoughts**
- **helps inspire your thoughts with reference to what you really want to write about**
- **helps remove the cobwebs from your brain**

You will build upon this technique throughout the workbook as you develop your memoir. As you use this technique to get your thoughts down on paper, you will soon develop your own personal style of bubbling.

Example:

Read the words in the example on the next page and see how my brain free-associated with the word 'tree'.

Note: Notice in the tree example how subsections started to develop, eg:

- **monkeys – jungle**
- **fresh – water**
- **autumn – leaves – green – spring**
- **bark – dogs**
- **wood – fire – campfire – Simon**
- **park – forest**
- **branch – brown**

- shade – night – stars
- climbing – tree house – brother

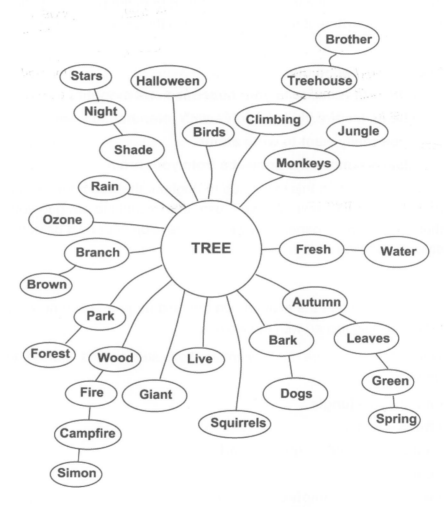

Notice from the following writing example how the word 'tree house' triggered thoughts of my brother, and how it became the focus of a memory from our lives together.

Example:

Title: My Big Brother

He wasn't a girl's guy but to me he was perfect. He was my big brother and I loved him totally. He took such pride in making things and even if he didn't always get them right, it didn't matter. At the tender age of 12 I became his assistant and would follow his every move, handing him nail after nail as he built a makeshift tree house from a discarded packing chest in the field at the back of our home.

Exercise A: Free-associate with the word 'sand' on the next page. Fill in the bubbles and continue creating your own bubbles. You can include as many bubble subsections as you want. Let your thoughts flow free and do not edit your work.

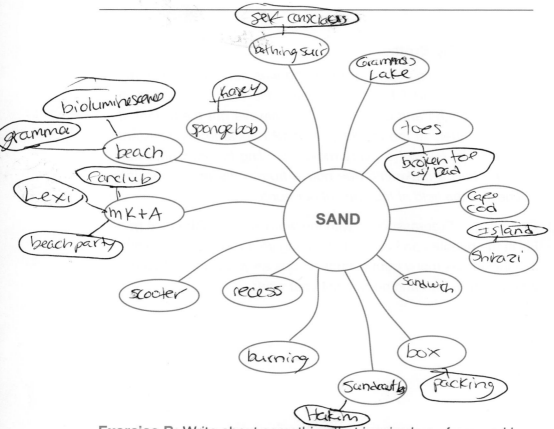

Exercise B: Write about something that inspired you from working on the bubbles. You may want to write something based on one or more of your 'sand' bubbles, or perhaps something totally different will come into your head as you start to write. Just write, do not edit your work. As you write, think of a title.

EXERCISE NUMBER: 3B

DATE: 2/20/21

TITLE: Bioluminescence.

The water lit up. I was a bit scared being in the Indian ocean on the coast of TZ, in the dark w/ no lifeguard, no safety net, no security, but my best friend. Nervous giggle turned to eruptions of pure joy as the moonlight interacted with the water in pure bio luminescent magic

Note: *You will notice as you develop your thoughts in this way that there are usually one or two bubbles that seem to really resonate with what you are thinking. It is as if they go 'bing' on the page.*

Work with these bubbles: they are clues, triggers to what you are really trying to say. These bubbles are important to your work: develop them. You can do this by putting the important word in a new central bubble on a new page. Start free-associating around it and you will develop your concept further. You can do this several times for each word or trigger that feels important to you.

A Writing Trick!

If at any stage your thoughts seem to come to a dead end when you are bubbling – if words suddenly cease to flow – read back over the last two or three bubbles, scratch them out, then reread the bubbles you drew before the bubbles you deleted and see what happens. Your thoughts will begin to flow again. To me, this dead end occurs when the brain reaches a fork in the road and chooses to go in the wrong direction. By returning to the point of indecision, you can easily go forward again in the right direction.

Checking Your Compass 2

Sensory Thinking   Exercise 4

Olfactory

How often do you stop to smell the flowers?

When was the last time you were really aware of a scent? When you are cooking, do you ever take a moment to engage in the delightful smell from a little jar of herbs?

Note 1: This exercise can be done by yourself, or ask someone to do it with you. If you are doing the exercise with another person, take it in turns to select the item for each other. Put the item in a bag to conceal it from the other person.

Note 2: The object of the exercise is not to name the item, but to engage with the smell and see what it evokes within you: perhaps a memory, a thought, a word, a person, a place, a colour – whatever comes to mind. Do not edit your thoughts.

Right-Brain Tip!

Remember: the left side of your brain will want to label the scent, to give it a name. The right side of your brain will engage in the 'feeling' element of the scent and what it evokes within you. Stay with your feelings; forget about *what* it is that you are sniffing.

Exercise A:

1. Search for an item with a really strong fragrance. It might be vinegar, mint sauce, tiger balm, perfume or coffee – anything that has a strong scent.

2. Close your eyes.

3. Smell the item.

4. Immediately bubble your thoughts below.

5. Create new bubbles as necessary; don't forget to include subsections if applicable.

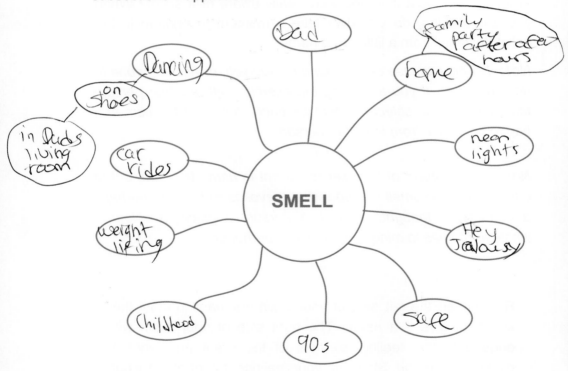

6. When you have finished bubbling, write a paragraph on the next page. You may write the paragraph based upon:

- **one of the words from your bubbles**
- **some of the words**
- **something completely different**

7. Title and date your work.

8. When complete, read your work.

There is no right way or wrong way

to do this exercise.

EXERCISE NUMBER: 4B

DATE: 2-20-21

TITLE: Dancing on Dad's Toes

Stand By Me is on the stereo, and I'm on my dad's toes as we dance. Family is around, but it feels like just us. I'm safe and joyful - so small, and protected and loved. The small front room is aglow, warm and cozy.

Note: From now on use the second sketch pad you packed for your writing journey to do all your bubble exercises. If you do this you will have a complete record of your thoughts through bubbles, in chronological order, as you go through the exercises in the workbook. This will provide you with easy access to your memories as you develop your memoir.

View from The Hilltop

Titles

In writing, the title should reflect an important element of the story.

We are very influenced by titles. We read books because we are attracted to their titles. We go to movies because we like their titles. Our senses expect certain tastes based on the names of dishes or the ingredients in food.

The names of characters in a story instantly give us a glimpse as to what to expect from the character. How differently we think of characters who are called Poppy or Anastasia, Dougie or Caesar! We give our friends pet names because they suit their character. Even when you are only using a working title for your writing, it will help differentiate your work from other pieces you may be writing at the same time.

As part of all the exercises in the workbook you will be asked to title each piece of writing. This is good practice in terms of becoming familiar with titling your work.

A Writing Trick!

If you can't think of a title, use The Bubble Technique to brainstorm possibilities, using a word or words as the starting point. In the central bubble, write a clue for yourself based on the concept of your story. If, for example, you are writing about a vacation you had with friends during a particular summer, write the name of the place and the year (eg 'Boston in 1988') in the central bubble, and let your thoughts flow from there.

Choosing Your Path

Unique Writing Voice

You will start writing creatively when you find

your unique writing voice.

As writers we are seeking to find our 'unique writing voice'. We each have a unique singing voice, and it is the same when we write. Our writing voice is how we individually express our experiences.

Imagine a group of people standing on the platform of a train station. They all board the same train, at the same time, and they are all going to the same destination. This group of people are all on the same journey, but their individual experiences of that journey will be completely different. No two people will have the same experience on that train or on that journey. Similarly, while a group of people can share the same family, event or disaster, each person's expression of that experience will be different. How we express our thoughts and experiences in writing is equally individual – it is our unique writing voice.

The more we write, the closer we get to finding our unique writing voice, and the stronger our voice becomes. From my workshop experiences, I believe that it is when you find your unique writing voice – the voice that expresses in a heartfelt way what it is you *want* to say – that is the moment you really start to write creatively.

47

The exercises throughout this workbook will help you become aware of and enhance your unique writing voice. Do not be afraid to experiment!

A Writing Tip!

As an experiment, and when you are a little further into the workbook, pick an exercise (a sensory exercise is very good for this) and if you can, ask a family member or a friend to do the same exercise with you at the same time. Then read your paragraphs to each other. Notice how completely different your writings are. This is a classic example of how two people experience the same thing at the same time, yet their individual experiences are totally different. It shows how each of us has a unique writing voice.

Tone of Voice

Coupled with finding your writing voice is the tone of how you say things. It is really important to remember from the first time you pick up your pen that no one wants to read what has become known as the 'misery memoir', the "Oh, poor me, look what happened to me in my life" book. It's boring; it makes you into a victim. It seeks revenge on those you feel have wronged you. It makes for miserable reading.

The tone of your writing should not be self-pitying, vengeful or whiney. Do you ever feel like listening to someone when they are moaning? No! And you won't want to read their book either!

48

You can find the tone that suits the topic you are dealing with and change it as you write your memoir. Every day our experiences of life are different, and you can express those differences in a tone that matches the experiences you are writing about. Your tone can change from sad to humorous, to serious and even angry. Be as entertaining as you possibly can. Be sensitive.

You are telling your story – no one else can tell it like you can. It is like having a deep objective conversation with your best friend about your life, how it evolved and how it brought you to the place you are in today. Your memoir should be written with authority as you unfold with objectivity the events of your life.

A Writing Tip!

I suggest that if you are writing your memoir for therapy – which is perfectly OK, and a great thing to do – don't write it with the expectation of getting published. This will mentally limit you and your work. If you don't think about publication, you will be able to be more honest with yourself and in your writing; you will be able to maintain your privacy. This may be more therapeutic for you, and you will probably obtain more peace from what you are writing about. I would also suggest that in some of the exercises you make a mental note, before you begin, to be as objective about your subject matter as you can, and see what difference it makes to your writing. Try this as often as you can; it may help a lot.

A Writing Trick!

Sometimes in writing it helps to visualise a person you want to tell your story to. Do this every time you write; it will help you find the way you want to tell your story, and will keep the tone of your story authentic.

Observe The Sights

Point of View (POV)

Memoir writing is always written in the first person.

Unlike fiction writing, where you have a choice about the *Point of View* (POV) from which you write (first person, third person limited narrative or the third person omniscient), in memoir writing there is no choice. In memoir writing you always write in the first person.

The very fact that you are writing a story from your own life – you were there, the story happened to you, you experienced it – means that you are automatically *in* the story, you are telling it, and therefore it is written in the first person.

You will be using the pronouns I, he, she.

Example: First Person

Title: Auto Lessons

My brother was six years older than me. His sureness about life made me feel safe and his sense of adventure made me feel alive. From as young as I can remember he was always fixing things – cars, bikes, tyres, model planes, lawnmowers – just about anything that had an engine or moved. He never gave up on anything; if he couldn't fix it he would put it aside until he figured out what to do with it. He never threw anything out. His collection of things that never got fixed just became bigger as he got older. He was a major squirrel.

All of those hours, days, months and years throughout his short life were spent learning from Dad, with Dad learning from him. They were like brothers together, absorbed in every detail of the engine and the problem – endless conversations that were way above my head. Endless conversations that excluded everyone else, even my mother, which I sensed upset her a lot. As a child, and even as a teenager, I would sit on the sidelines and listen, surrounded by engine parts, insanely bored with the conversations but just happy to be there with the two of them. I reckon most of the time they didn't even know I was there at all; such was the intensity of their relationship and the problem in question.

Those memories come flooding back to me every time I bring my car to a garage – when the garage guy inevitably looks at me with a twinkle of great curiosity as I discuss the depth and diagnostics of engine repair with such ease and understanding!

Tense

The tense of the story is important. It is also a part of finding your unique writing voice, which will become easier as you do the exercises and change the tenses around. You will sometimes write in the present tense, sometimes in the past tense, and even use the future tense to ponder about what will happen in your story.

Longitude and Latitude

Showing *and* Telling

One of the differences between fiction writing and memoir writing is that in fiction writing you show your readers how the story evolves, while memoir writing is about showing and telling.

When you write fiction the story evolves by putting the characters in conflict with one another and showing the readers their actions and reactions to the plot. Memoir writing is quite different: you not only *show* the reader what has taken place but you also *tell* the reader the effect the action had on you, the writer of the story. You can ponder over actions and the effects they had at the time and thereafter; you can also contemplate the event in detail and the impact it had on the people around you. Thus memoir writing is about showing *and* telling.

Study the two examples on the next page. Notice how in the fiction writing example the message is 'shown' through story action. In the memoir example the incident is revealed by showing my reaction to the phone call, as I told the reader the impact it had upon my life.

Example: Fiction Writing

SHOWING

The phone rang too many times. Amy was too busy joking with her office mates to bother about something as real as work. Still laughing, she finally lifted the receiver, her gaze fixed upon Ryan as she teased his call of the wild with her big green eyes. Suddenly her bubbly and confident manner changed as she flung the phone across the room. The smashing of the black plastic against the sparkling white walls instantly shattered the atmosphere that had existed only moments previously, like the sound of deep ice cracking in the centre of a lake when the thaw of spring sets in.

Example: Memoir Writing

SHOWING and TELLING

The impact of that phone call would change my life forever. A group of vowels, consonants and letters strung together into one short sentence by a voice which even to this day belonged to I don't know who. One minute I was a happy-go-lucky 24-year-old in love with life, excited about my Friday evening and weekend of partying with my friends. The next I was instantly alone in the world in a way that separated me from everything that I had known, felt and understood until that moment in time.

The crashing and smashing of the phone on the far office wall as I hurled that lump of plastic across the room mirrored the surge of pain that ripped through every muscle and vein in my body. My big brother was dead, my one and only, my hero, my truest connection to the world. In an instant everything had changed and my life from that moment would never be the same again.

Comment

Notice the tone in my writing voice: there is no moaning or whining, it is reflective, looking back on an event that was significant, telling it how it was.

As you progress through the workbook you will have many opportunities to express your writing voice as you show and tell your memories.

Reading The Map

Ingredients of Memoir Writing

You have to know the rules

before you can break the rules.

In this workbook you will discover how to write your memoir and what it is you need to think about in order to do so. When you've completed the workbook, you will understand the elements and the principles of memoir writing. You will then understand how to *think* like a writer because you will know the rules.

As in all writing, there are guidelines and principles to memoir writing. You have to know the rules before you can break the rules. When you understand the rules you are then in a position to be creative with your thoughts and you will know and understand how to structure your work – to make it personal. You will be able to tell your story in the way that you want to tell it.

So think of the rules of memoir as the ingredients in a cake recipe. If you leave something out, the cake won't rise, or it will not taste good. It is like this in writing. If you leave an ingredient out the story won't work; it will be flat on the page and will not interest the reader.

This workbook builds upon the ingredients of memoir in easy stages, allowing you to understand what you need to think about, and teaching you how to mix all of the ingredients together.

You will learn how to make your story not only work, but work in an interesting way.

The Ingredients of Memoir Writing

1. Memories

Recall what you remember.

Evoke forgotten experiences.

2. Characters

Include the people who made a difference.

3. Settings

Create atmosphere.

4. Theme

Unearth your subject matter.

Identify your theme.

5. Truth

Tell it like it was.

6. Structure

Define the way to tell your story.

7. Language

Use evocative language.

Now study The Memoir Map on the following page and become familiar with the elements of memoir writing.

In the next section of the workbook you will explore each element of The Memoir Map in detail, step by step, as you discover how to translate your life experiences and memories into creatively writing your memoir.

The Memoir Map
Your Writing Journey

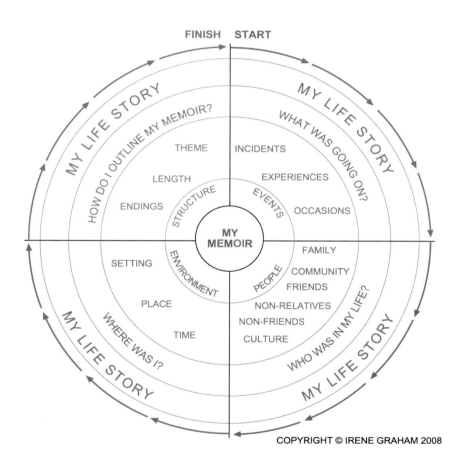

FINISH   START

MY LIFE STORY

MY LIFE STORY

MY LIFE STORY

MY LIFE STORY

HOW DO I OUTLINE MY MEMOIR?

WHAT WAS GOING ON?

WHERE WAS I?

WHO WAS IN MY LIFE?

THEME

INCIDENTS

LENGTH

EXPERIENCES

ENDINGS

STRUCTURE

EVENTS

OCCASIONS

MY MEMOIR

FAMILY

SETTING

ENVIRONMENT

PEOPLE

COMMUNITY

FRIENDS

PLACE

NON-RELATIVES

NON-FRIENDS

TIME

CULTURE

PART 3
Planning Your Journey
Section 1: Events

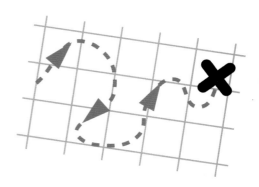

The Memoir Map
Events: WHAT WAS GOING ON?

You are now embarking upon the North East
route of your writing journey.

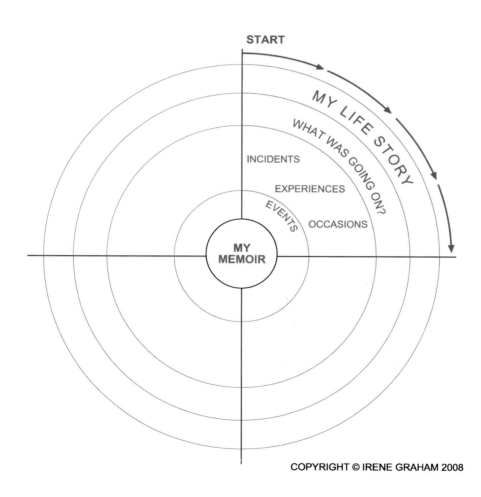

START

MY LIFE STORY

WHAT WAS GOING ON?

INCIDENTS

EXPERIENCES

EVENTS

OCCASIONS

MY
MEMOIR

65

Connecting to Your Path 3

Free Drawing   Exercise 5

Draw what you are feeling right now...with your *left hand.*

Whether you are right-hand dominant or left-hand dominant, use your *left hand* to do this exercise.

Use only chalk or crayons, not pens or pencils.

Use your drawing sketch pad for this exercise.

Remember: try to depict your feelings through symbols and patterns, which means you are using your right brain.

Title and date your work – with your *left hand.*

Right-Brain Tip!

Your right brain dominates your left hand. By using your left hand to draw you are exercising your right brain. Become aware of how different this feels (if you are right hand dominant).

Paste your Photograph
for
Exercise 6
here

Checking Your Compass 3

Sensory Thinking   Exercise 6

> *Visual*
>
> *Photographs evoke memories and help*
>
> *us to recall details of the past.*

A photograph is a moment from a life. Photographs speak to us, allowing us to recall moments and periods in time with a person or a group of people. They are a powerful way to evoke memories and stories, and help you to explore your visual senses.

Exercise A:

1. Select a photograph from your family album, or one that is hanging on your wall, or in your computer or phone. Make a hard copy of the image if you can.

2. Study the photograph and recall all the memories it brings back to you: the time it was taken, the details of the person or people in the image. Remember everything you can about that particular time, the memories and stories that the image evokes.

3. Go to your bubble sketch pad and bubble everything you can remember about this photo. Paste the photo into your workbook, or keep it beside you as you work on the bubbles.

4. Write a paragraph about the photograph.

5. Title and date your work.

6. When complete, read your work.

There is no right or wrong way
to do this exercise.

Example:

Study of a school photograph of my brother, aged 12, sitting in front of a school map.

Title: The Ancient Way

The map was torn and worn, the coated plastic paper cracking more every time Miss Jones stood on her tippy toes and reached for the broken string on the roller above the blackboard, pulling the ancient map of Ireland into focus. I doubt she even noticed the condition of it. If she did that was never apparent, but then emotion was not her thing.

Miss Jones was very proud of this map. It seemed to give her a sense of authority as she banged the end of her thick chipped wooden ruler against each of the 32 counties in Ireland, one by one, harshly demanding each of us in turn to read the name in Irish and repeat it in English. I always got it right because I became familiar with her system of pointing and asking the same questions, as she systemically moved around the map. It was very left-brained of her!

Note: *Even though this photo was of my brother, the map in the background of the image evoked memories and images of my own school days.*

A Writing Tip!

This exercise can be repeated over and over to recall memories of people, places and times in your life. It is a powerful tool for dipping into your well of memory.

Finding The Well I

Recalling Memories   **Exercise 7**

Uncover your well of memory; unearth the details of your significant memories.

Memorabilia plays an enormous part in our lives. It is made up of all sorts of weird and wonderful things, precious and priceless. Twigs, stones, clothes, images, a letter, a hankie, paintings, jewellery, doodles, fabric, a lock of hair, a piece of glass – just about anything can be memorabilia. What I love most about memorabilia is that a letter could be the most precious possession a person owns because of the memories that surround it, while on their wall hangs a priceless oil painting.

Memorabilia: objects collected as souvenirs of important personal events or experiences

Exercise A:

1. Select a piece of memorabilia from your life, a significant item that holds a lot of memories for you.

2. Really study this item, recalling the memories it brings you. What images come to mind as you look at it?

3. Hold the object in your hands, close your eyes and become aware of the feelings it evokes. What do you remember from the time when this item became important to you?

4. In your bubble sketch pad, bubble everything you can

remember about your special item. Keep the item beside you as you work on the bubbles.

5. Write a paragraph about it.

6. Title and date your work.

7. When complete, read your work.

Pausing at The Well I

Evoking Memories   Exercise 8

Your well of memory is filled with magical times as well as
the moments that challenged you in your life journey.

At this point in your writing journey you are seeking to tap into your well of memory, to uncover and explore the significant memories of events that make up your individual life story.

Each life comprises a series of events, occasions and experiences that in some way are all connected to one another. These make up the whole of our lives. All the incidents and experiences of your life have brought you to where you are today.

As you progress through the workbook, you will build upon your memories and experiences step by step. Enjoy each exercise as you write; you are in no rush, there is no time limit.

By navigating slowly through your writing journey using The Memoir Map as your guide, you will automatically start recalling various life memories.

This map and the following exercises will help you to define and focus upon the events in your life that you want to write about.

Keep it simple. Do not feel you have to dig or delve deep into your psyche. Let your thoughts flow freely, and have fun while doing the following exercises.

Exercise A:

1. Think of as many occasions, events or experiences as you can that happened in your life prior to the age of 15, regardless of how insignificant they seem.

Think of occasions that were:

- *trivial*
- *serious*
- *funny*
- *challenging*
- *life changing*
- *awkward*

2. In your bubble sketch pad, name as many of the occasions as you can remember – through bubbling, not writing, eg:

- *the time I fell into cement*
- *my travels to school on my own*
- *the summer I discovered canoeing*
- *discovering the differences between me and my family*
- *learning to ride a bike*
- *getting drunk*
- *questioning my faith*
- *the night Gordon kissed me*

Exercise B:

1. Focus upon one particular occasion that you bubbled about.

2. Go to a new bubble page in your bubble sketch pad and bubble in detail about this occasion. Include:

- *places*
- *people*
- *dialogue*
- *anything you can remember about it*

3. Write a paragraph in the first person, present tense, about this occasion. In other words, write the paragraph as if the occasion was taking place right now.

4. Title and date your work.

5. When complete, read your work.

Exercise C:

1. Rewrite the paragraph in the first person, past tense.

2. You are now looking back on the occasion, writing about how it happened.

3. Title and date your work.

4. When complete, read your work.

A Writing Tip!

Read your writing aloud to another person if you feel comfortable doing so. This really helps to build confidence. Pick a person who you know will encourage, not criticise you.

Checking Your Compass 4

Sensory Thinking   **Exercise 9**

Touch

As with our other senses, the sense of touch is different for each person. The signals our nerve endings send to our brains are very individual, determining our personal realities.

The ideal way to do this exercise is with another person, but it is easily done on your own – if you stay in your right brain!

Note: As mentioned previously, sensory exercises are not about guessing what the item is that you are exploring – that is left-brain thinking. Instead, these exercises are about connecting to what the item triggers for you emotionally and the images it evokes for you.

Note: We all react in different ways to things that we are unsure about. This can bring up deep unknown fears within. If you are doing this exercise with another person, make sure the item you choose for them to touch will not upset them, eg something slimy or something that could bite!

77

Exercise A:

1. Choose an item to touch. It might be fabric, a pine cone, wool or even a leaf – something that has a strong texture. Be imaginative in your choice.

2. If you are doing this exercise with another person, put the item in a bag.

3. Close your eyes and feel the item with your *left hand*. See what images it brings to mind, what memories it evokes. Stay in your right brain; do not try to figure out what it is you are touching.

4. Go to your bubble sketch pad and bubble everything that you associate with this item.

5. Write a paragraph. You may write something that touching the item brought to mind, or you may write something apparently unconnected that suddenly comes to mind.

6. Title and date your work.

7. When complete, read your work.

There is no right or wrong way
to do this exercise.

Right-Brain Tip!

Our left brain controls objective, precise language. It is good at naming things. Feeling the item with your left hand (which sends signals to the right side of the brain) allows you to stay more with the feeling element of the item, as opposed to trying to name it.

What Route is Best?

Time Lines   Exercise 10

A Time Line, often used in therapy, can be used creatively

as a visual representation to chart your memoir

and your life story.

I was very excited when I first encountered Time Lines. I was even more excited when I worked out how to use them creatively in my writing. Time Lines, like bubbling, are another form of focusing thoughts which will allow you to direct your writing without having to write much. Time Lines are the maps of your subconscious; they represent another form of visual thinking.

Think of Time Lines as the blueprint of your life.

- **Where are you coming from?**
- **What did you do, and when?**
- **Where are you going to?**
- **How are you going to get there?**

You will build upon the uses of Time Lines as you progress through the workbook and work upon your memoir.

Note: Time lines don't necessarily have to be formed in chronological order. Note events and ages at random if that is easier.

Your Time Line will serve as the foundation for your writing – the blueprint of your life.

TIME LINE EXAMPLE

Age		Event
4	•	moved house
4	•	first day at school
12	•	fighting with a teacher
18	•	leaving home
12	•	my first kiss
22	•	death of my mother
24	•	death of my brother
24	•	changing careers
24	•	falling in love
24	•	moved house
24	•	taking care of my father
28	•	leaving Ireland

Note: Some people remember events in their life by age, others by the year they happened. Make the Time Line work for you – recall the events by age or year, whichever you find easiest.

The Time Line could include any event in your life, eg:

- **births of children**
- **marriages**
- **divorces**
- **career moments**
- **illnesses**
- **learning to drive**
- **travels**

Note: *The Time Line can include anything – from simple memories to bigger events that were more significant.*

A Writing Tip!

Take as much time over this exercise as possible. From it you will uncover all sorts of events and happenings in your life that you may have forgotten about. Be honest with yourself – remember, you don't have to reveal what you write.

Exercise A:

Answer the following question using the sample Time Line overleaf.

- **What age were you when significant events took place in your life?**

Note your age and event on the Time Line, as shown in the example. Recreate your own Time Line taking as much space as you need to complete this exercise.

TIMELINE

Age or Year	Event
Oct 30, 1990	birth
5 y/o 1995	parents divorce
	move to Bellingham
	meet Veronica
1996	start school - Stallbrook
	mom + Charlie together
1998	meet Rachel Courthy
	start sax, track/soccer
2003	maunt!
	First period on First day
	meet Amy Horan!
~~2004~~	an all HS friends
	Rose best friend + - not friends
2004	First colonoscopy
2006	Ireland! first trip abroad
	dad + Lori divorce
	Arizona service trip
2007	Lynch syndrome diagnosis
2008	Toronto w/ band
	NCAS tutoring
~~2009~~ 2009	Graduate High school
	work for cutco + Furgery
	start Stonehill
	mom hysterectomy
summer	Start + college @ Stonehill
	Lose 70 lbs
	became atheist
	- Philos + religion
	meet KKel

Biggest change #

Dahlin
e

82

2010   • suite! Cascino 2nd North   meet
     cutting, lose weight CW
    • ~~Insanity~~
sure research   • sara friendship strengthens
w/ matthew → meet Hailey   Habitat to
+ wetzel   **2011** • run clubs   SC — Emany
     media relations
    • study abroad Italy
    • first real kiss Ahmed Prague

2012 • Kenya!   swahili   Odooks + com
     Date dred   Donna + Health + com
    • research — amazing! Rhetoric
    • host fam, Brian, music

2013 • Hot mess   Lola passed
     GRADUATE   Religious epiphany
    • Gramma passed
     BACKPACKING
    • start musician corps — move to NC
    • meet Kelly — fall in love 1st time
     Live w/ Autumn … + Jacquie
2014 • TANZANIA
2015 • Tanzania   Solo — Kevin …
2016/7 • IHP   2 trip to EA   Harvard → depression, appendectomy
2018 • Hakim -love, loss, leave, move
2019 • IHP, kickboxing, mary
2020 • IHP → Pandemic → home →
                 Gabriele + Dar

You have now completed a Time Line. Well done!

You can, and should, return to it at any point to develop it further.

Looking into The Well I

Including Memories   Exercise 11

Look deep into your well of memory – it will enable you to recall the times in your life that made a difference.

As discussed in the last chapter, your Time Line is the foundation for your writing – the blueprint of your life. The process is similar to building a house. The architect designs the building and then works from a blueprint of his drawings to instigate the build and develop the plans. Your Time Line is your architect's drawing; from here you will be able to build upon your writing and develop what you want to write about.

You will now develop your blueprint further.

You may want to do the following exercise in private and choose to keep it private.

Exercise A:

1. Reread your Time Line in Exercise 10A.

Answer the following question:

   • **What age were you when the most significant change took place in your life?**

Note the age on the left column of your Time Line. How many

entries do you have at a given age? This will probably answer the question for you. If there are several significant ages, pick one to begin with that you feel comfortable with.

2. Go to your bubble sketch pad. Put your age in the central bubble. Bubble everything you can remember about being that age. Include people, places, events and experiences.

Use the following questions to initiate your work:

- **What age were you?**
- **What was going on in your life?**
- **What were you struggling with?**
- **What did you look like?**
- **What did you feel like?**
- **What were you hoping for?**
- **What were you avoiding?**
- **What did you discover?**

3. Write a paragraph in the first person, present tense about that time.

4. Title and date your work.

5. Now write a paragraph in the first person, past tense about that time. Reflect upon it as you see it now, including these thoughts in your writing.

6. Title and date your work.

7. When complete, read your work.

A Writing Tip!

This exercise can be done over and over and over. It is a powerful way to recall memories. For the purpose of developing your writing and your understanding of memoir, work on the above question until you find the age you want to write about and then progress to the next exercise. At this stage, do *not* get stuck in writing about every age.

Drinking from The Well I

Developing Memories   Exercise 12

Imbibe the moment – the minute details that made

a difference to your life journey.

You may want to do the following exercise in private and choose to keep it private.

To develop your blueprint further, complete the following:

Exercise A:

1. Reread your Time Line in Exercise 10A.

Answer the following question:

• **What was the most significant happening or event that changed your life?**

You may or may not have already recalled this event on your Time Line. What you are seeking to answer here is a defined event: a moment that changed your life. There could be several events that changed your life. At this stage define the most significant one.

This particular question is sometimes a hard and difficult question to answer. It can take courage to be truthful, even with yourself, to answer this question.

I believe that getting in touch with the answer to this question is the true foundation upon which to build a major life story.

When I initially started to facilitate writing workshops, I asked this question a lot. It astonished me the profound reactions I got from participants. Responses vary on many levels: death of a loved one, lost love, birth of a child, marriage, finding birth parents, abuse, divorce, admitting addiction, finding faith, and even not telling the truth about something significant, which ultimately changed lives as well.

So reread your Time Line and ask yourself this question. You probably know the answer already. Remember, you do not have to share your answers with anyone. Once you complete this exercise you can work with the answer in many ways in your writing. So to repeat:

- **What was the most significant happening or event that changed your life?**

2. Find a quiet space where you will not be interrupted and make yourself comfortable. Go to your bubble sketch pad. Put this question in the central bubble and start bubbling around it. Include anything that comes to mind, free-flowing with your answer. Take your time.

3. Then write as much as you can for as long as you can about this time in your life. Do not edit your work. Do not worry about tense or grammar. Just keep writing.

4. Title and date your work.

5. When complete, read your work.

Your route is becoming defined; the foundation for your writing is finding its course. Keep going. Do not edit or judge your work.

Connecting to Your Path 4

Free Drawing   Exercise 13

Draw anything with your *left hand.*

Whether you are right-hand dominant or left-hand dominant, use your *left hand* to do the above exercise.

Use only chalk or crayons, not pens or pencils.

Use your drawing sketch pad for this exercise.

Draw anything; do not pre-decide what it is you are going to draw.

Let your left hand guide you, follow it, and see what happens.

Connect to what you are drawing and ask yourself what it means to you. As you draw, think of a title for your work.

Title and date your work – with your *left hand.*

Looking Back 1

Congratulate yourself! You have now completed the North East section of your writing journey.

You have recalled and remembered many events, occasions and experiences in your life.

You have developed just a few of them, but now you know how to develop *all* of them, if you want to, when you want to.

You have still not reached your destination and you do not know yet how to get there. There are still paths to follow and ways to approach your life that will show you what you want to write about, so keep going forward. That is what is most important right now.

Enjoy your journey. Getting started is always the hardest task, and now you have done that. Look back on your work and see how far you have come.

**Well done! You are now well on the writing road.
It is important to keep going forward.**

A Writing Tip!

Reread your exercises and consider all the things you have not only remembered, but learned. As you progress in your writing, start listening to and be conscious of your unique writing voice. Be aware of how your writing is developing; be mindful of writing in the first person and the tense that you are writing in, past or present.

PART 3

Planning Your Journey

Section 2: People

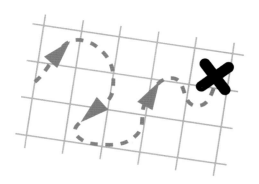

91

The Memoir Map

People: WHO WAS IN MY LIFE?

You are now embarking upon the South East

route of your writing journey

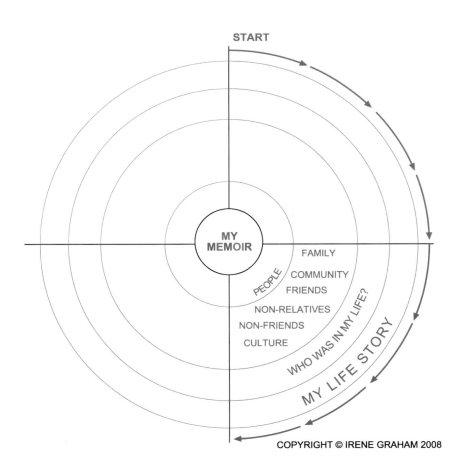

Checking Your Compass 5

Sensory Thinking   Exercise 14

Taste

Our sense of taste can be alive or

virtually non-existent.

This sensory thinking exercise allows you to explore the sense of taste. As many people suffer from food allergies, it is better to select the item yourself that you want to use in this exercise.

Find a food item or a sweet that will make your taste buds tingle, eg sherbet, or something sour, or something hot like chillies. You could even select a food item that you don't like the taste of.

This exercise is about connecting to what the item triggers for you emotionally and the images it evokes within.

Note: *If you are doing this exercise with another person make sure to check if they have any allergies or reactions to certain types of food. This is very important.*

Exercise A:

1. Select the food product or sweet you want to taste.

2. Close your eyes.

3. Place the food item on your tongue.

4. Be aware of what the taste feels like. Be conscious of the

images it evokes within you, and the memories it brings to mind.

5. Take your time. Slowly let your taste buds talk to you.

6. Go to your bubble sketch pad and bubble everything that you associate with this taste.

7. Write a paragraph. You may write something that was evoked when tasting the item, or something apparently unconnected.

8. Title and date your work.

9. When complete, read your work.

There is no right or wrong way
to do this exercise.

Right-Brain Tip!

This is a fun exercise to do over and over and is great for developing your right brain. Even when you are cooking, take a moment to taste something in the kitchen and see what images it brings to mind.

Searching for The Atmosphere

Tone and Mood   Exercise 15

It is the tone and mood of your writing voice that

contributes to the atmosphere of your memoir.

As mentioned previously in 'Choosing your Path/Unique Writing Voice', the tone of your writing voice should reflect the experience you are writing about – without being self-pitying, vengeful or whiney.

It is your frame of mind – your *attitude* about a particular event or occasion – that influences how you write about it.

Example:

Title: The Singing Lesson

He grabbed the top of my arm in rage. Feelings of indignation engulfed me like a pot boiling over and I knew even at 12 this was something a teacher was not allowed to do, or would ever do to me and get away with it. His long red bulbous nose seemed to increase in size and deepen in colour as he squeezed my arm tighter, yelling at me to go to the back of the choir because I was a dreadful singer. His words stung like a bee eating into my bellybutton and enraged me further. I landed a karate chop with the full force of my hand on his grip, yelling at him to let me go. There was total silence in the classroom

Don't be wishing

attitude influences word choice

Practice this often to enhance writing voice

as this scene of defiance erupted. I had become the scapegoat for a room of students that were afraid of this hideous man.

Comment

Notice the rage in my words, the temper I felt when this happened. Not only did this teacher insult me but he hurt my feelings.

Exercise A:

1. Return to Exercise 8A in your bubble sketch pad. Select another occasion, event or experience that happened to you prior to the age of 15.

2. Think of the *mood* you were in when this event took place in your life. Were you happy? Sad? Angry? Confident? Devastated? Worried? Confused? Distraught? Frightened? Amused?

3. Write a paragraph about this event, showing through your writing your attitude, feelings and mood *at that time.*

4. Title and date your work.

5. When complete, read your work.

Note: *You can practise this exercise over and over using different situations, expressing a different mood and tone each time in your writing.*

Right-Brain Tip!

Take a quiet moment to think about this exercise before you start putting words on the page. Think of the occasion you want to return to and write about. Recall and remember the *feeling* of what you felt as you experienced this particular event or occasion in your life. This *feeling* will really help you to translate, communicate and express that time though your writing. This is a powerful way to enhance and deepen your writing voice.

Enjoying The View

The Retrospective Voice   Exercise 16

Reflection upon your experiences will bring about the

retrospective voice in your writing.

An important ingredient in memoir writing is your ability to reflect upon your life and communicate this reflective observation to your reader. Reflection is like the binding ingredient in baking a cake – too much or too little will have a completely different effect upon the outcome.

Reflective consideration in your writing requires observation and deep introspection as you, the hero or heroine, stand outside your story and look back with wisdom and objectivity, viewing in your mind what you feel was actually going on. You are viewing the facts of each given event as you knew them, seeking in retrospect to understand what was then unknown to you. As part of the memoir writing process, you communicate your feelings and attitude towards these happenings, and the consequential effects that they have had upon your life – *through your retrospective voice.*

You are looking at how your life evolved and the sense you made – and now make – of the events that shaped it.

A huge part of memoir writing is how you view your life story *now*, as you contemplate upon your experiences.

Therefore, the *attitude* of your retrospective voice, which is expressed through the tone and mood of your reflections, relates to how objective you are about the event that you are writing about. Think about how you feel. Can you find an amusing, good-humoured or light-hearted voice to relate to the event, or even an ironic voice? You may also find your retrospective voice in being just deeply thoughtful, which will show the reader that you have a mature, contemplative attitude towards your life.

I think reflection not only requires great objectivity, but deep honesty about your feelings, as you remain the observer with the ability to ponder and muse about your life and the events you are writing about.

Introspection is possible at any age; you do not have to wait until you are several decades old to undergo a process of self-examination into your own feelings, thoughts and motives towards events in your life.

Introspection will bring about clarity in your writing and the reader will subsequently identify with the substance of your story on a much deeper level.

Note: *The retrospective voice is like the second voice in your memoir – the mature voice of objectivity and wisdom that is spoken through the mood and tone of your writing as you convey your story.*

Read the following paragraph as quoted previously in the chapter 'Observe the Sights/Point of View', example: Auto Lessons – noting the highlighted sentences.

Example:

Title: Auto Lessons

My brother was six years older than me. His sureness about life made me feel safe and his sense of adventure made me feel alive. From as young as I can remember he was always fixing things – cars, bikes, tyres, model planes, lawnmowers – just about anything that had an engine or moved. He never gave up on anything; if he couldn't fix it he would put it aside until he figured out what to do with it. He never threw anything out. His collection of things that never got fixed just became bigger as he got older. He was a major squirrel.

*All of those hours, days, months and years throughout his short life were spent learning from Dad, with Dad learning from him. They were like brothers together, absorbed in every detail of the engine and the problem – endless conversations that were way above my head. Endless conversations that excluded everyone else, even my mother, **which I sensed upset her a lot**. As a child, and even as a teenager, I would sit on the sidelines and listen, surrounded by engine parts, insanely bored with the conversations but just happy to be there with the two of them. **I reckon most of the time they didn't even know I was there at all; such was the intensity of their relationship and the problem in question.***

Those memories come flooding back to me every time I bring my car to a garage – when the garage guy inevitably looks at me with a twinkle of great curiosity as I discuss the depth and diagnostics of engine repair with such ease and understanding!

Note 1: *The retrospective voice in the above example is highlighted. It is my reflection, in hindsight, as to what I think was really going on. The retrospective voice in this instance is interspersed between sentences throughout the writing.*

Note 2: *Another way to use the retrospective voice is to clearly define the story in one paragraph, then write another paragraph referring to your story in reflective hindsight, before switching again to the story.*

Note 3: *Another way to access the retrospective voice is to write a complete chapter, then at the end of the chapter write your reflections with regard to the subject matter in your retrospective voice.*

Comment

The mood of my retrospective voice was thoughtful. The tone of my writing voice at the end of the last paragraph was playful.

Note: *Reread the above examples so that you understand the three ways to incorporate the retrospective voice into your writing. Connect with each writing example and ask yourself which type of retrospective voice resonates with you.*

Exercise A:

1. Reread the paragraph you wrote in Exercise 15A.

2. Write a new paragraph about this memory in the first person, present tense – as if you were experiencing it now.

3. Now write another paragraph about this memory in the past tense – looking back on it from an adult prospective. Include your retrospective voice in your writing. Before you write,

decide how you will include your retrospective voice, based on the above options.

4. Title and date your work.

5. Reread your work and decide which paragraph your writing was the strongest in. What tense did you relate to in your writing? Did you get a sense of incorporating your retrospective voice into your writing?

A Writing Tip!

This very powerful exercise helps to evoke and strengthen your writing voice as you develop tense, POV and retrospective voice within your writing. Repeat this exercise often while developing your work, using each way to express your retrospective voice. This exercise provides the key to finding the *voices* in which you want to write your memoir.

Finding The Well 2

Recalling People   Exercise 17

In your well of memory reside the people that made

a difference and influenced your life.

You are now ready to interact and build upon another level of your memories. You are more aware of your life story and have documented many events, occasions and experiences that were significant to you in your life.

These events, occasions and memories that you have created in your bubbles and on your Time Lines will form the basis of your bedrock material for your memoir. You should refer to them often.

As you reread your work, you will automatically remember other elements that you omitted. Continue to free-associate with these memories and your work to date; this is how you will build upon your life story and find what you are seeking to include in your memoir.

You will now recall the people that were in your life, the people that made a difference and influenced you, the people that had an effect upon you. They are the people who were important to you, the people that inspired you or defeated you.

how to inc ppl. in Story
imp to write you into story
+ develop who you were

**Exercise A:**

1. Reread your bubbles from Exercise 8A, regarding events in your life prior to age 15. Pick one event from the bubbles that you want to develop further. Choose a happy incident from your childhood, one that you look back upon and smile about.

Read the following example:

Title: Quicksand

I knew that day, like so many other days, that it was a close call whether I would make the 3pm bus home or not. If I missed this bus it meant waiting an hour for the next one and Mum would be annoyed with me again. I enjoyed being in Karen's house so much after school that time always went by far too quickly. Her house was so different to mine; there always seemed to be an abundance of people in it, there were so many things to do and the food they ate was not what I ate at home. Her mum was a hairdresser and she let us play in the salon. Karen never made the journey to my house; it was just too far away. It was another reason, at the ripe age of 10, that I hated living in the country.

I ran and ran so that I would make the bus, doing my best to ignore how much my new brown laced shoes hurt. Panting, I looked up, and on the other side of the river I saw the bus. I figured I could still make it if I ran that bit harder across the bridge which was now in front of me. It was a challenge but if the traffic on the other side of the river was slow, which it usually was, I would get to the bus stop before the bus did. As I dashed across the road between cars I encountered a workman's barrier, one of those red tape things to keep people out. I ducked under it, and low and behold I was sucked into wet cement, right up my knees, like quicksand. Blushing and humiliated I looked around for help, the bus and my mother's annoyance now far from my thoughts.

2. Now think of the person you were then at the time of your chosen event. Focus upon the following questions:

- **What age were you?**
- **What was going on in your life?**
- **What did you look like?**
- **What did you feel like – happy/confident/jealous/excited/ curious?**
- **What were you wearing?**
- **What were you learning?**
- **What were you doing?**

3. Go to your bubble sketch pad. Bubble everything you can remember about yourself at this time in your life. Place the name of the incident in your central bubble. Refer to the questions above as a guideline. As you free-associate with the above questions, include in the bubbles anything else that you can remember about yourself from this time.

Exercise B:

1. Start a new bubble. Answer the following questions:

- **Name the significant people in your life at that time.**
- **What people were around you during the event?**

Include everyone you can remember. Name them as you referred to them at that stage of your life.

Exercise C:

1. Reread your bubbles from Exercise A and B above, then combine your thoughts and write a paragraph about this time in your life. Choose to write about it in the present or past tense. Try to find *humour* and *irony* in your writing voice as you relate to and write about this incident in your life.

2. Title and date your work.

3. When complete, read your work.

Well done. You are now developing ways to merge people with events and occasions. You are learning how to be specific and hone into the details of a particular time as you find your writing voice by *showing* the reader your feelings with regard to that time in your life.

Further Exercises:

Now go back to the original exercise (8A), or to an event on your Time Line, and choose another event that you want to develop, perhaps some event or occasion that contained more conflict. Repeat the above exercise.

Note: You can repeat this exercise over and over as you draw upon and define the occasions and events you want to include in your memoir, recalling and including the people that were important to you at various stages of your life.

Note: For the purpose of moving forward and learning to develop your writing further, don't get stuck with repeating the above exercise too often at this stage. Do it a few times for *practice, and then go on to the next exercise.*

> **A Writing Tip!**
>
> When you reread your bubbles, remember to notice what bubble goes 'bing' for you on the page. This is usually a clue that this element of your thoughts is important to you, and is a hint or trigger of a memory that you should consider developing further on a new page.

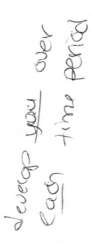

develop you over each time period

Pausing at The Well 2

Remembering People   Exercise 18

Define the special people in your life and remember

them in detail.

Whether you are writing creative non-fiction or fiction, stories are all about characters. They are the backbone of the story, the crucial element that conveys your narrative. Your story depends on how you develop your characters. Well-developed characters result in interesting, meaningful writing and make readers keep turning the pages.

Because you are the hero or heroine in your story, it is also important for you to develop *you* as the central character at different stages of your life, expressing who you were and what you were like with depth and power.

The more detail you recall about the people in your life *before* you start putting words on paper, the more vibrant and creative your writing will be. It is obvious in a story when the author is familiar with the people he or she is writing about. The reader can instantly relate to these characters, understanding, empathising and identifying with them.

The Bubble Technique really helps you to develop and recall the people in your life that were important to you. It helps you to bring back distant memories and details about them. Using The Bubble Technique also allows you to remember many facets of your own life and personality, enabling you to portray yourself as the hero or heroine of your story in a creative way.

Exercise A:

1. Reread your bubbles from Exercise 17B.

2. Answer the following question:

   • **Regarding the event you are writing about, who was the most important person to you at that time?**

3. Put the name of this person in the centre of a new bubble. Answer the following questions about him or her:

   • **What age or approximate age was this person?**

   • **What was their relationship to you? For example: mother/father/aunt/friend/best friend's mum etc.**

   • **What did they look like?**

   • **What sort of personality did they have?**

   • **Where did they live?**

   • **How often did you see them?**

   • **How did they make you feel?**

   • **What did you learn from them?**

   • **Were they kind to you or not?**

   • **What sort of clothes did they wear?**

   • **What impressed you about them?**

   • **What did you like about them?**

   • **What did you not like about them?**

   • **If they worked, what did they work at?**

   • **What were their hobbies?**

   • **What do you think they wanted from life?**

- How did they inspire you?
- Did they ever make you feel defeated? How?
- Did you like this person? Why? Why not?
- What adventures did you have with them?
- Did you laugh or cry with them?
- What were their hopes?
- What were their fears?
- What were their opinions?
- What conflicts did you have with this person?

As you free-associate with the above questions, include in the bubbles anything else you can remember about this person.

4. Write a paragraph about this person. See what emerges from thinking about them and recalling details regarding the influence they had upon your life.

5. Title and date your work.

6. When complete, read your work.

Note: There is no right or wrong way to do this exercise. You are starting to find your own writing style and are beginning to know and understand how to tap into and trigger memories.

A Writing Tip!

You can and should repeat this exercise for every person that you want to include in your memoir. It is a very powerful way to recall the people that were important to you in your life.

is multiple ppl = repeat exercise

Note: *You now have a greater understanding of how to develop the characters in your life that were important to you and your story. And from the last chapter, you also know how to develop you as the person that you were at a given point in your life.*

Note: *As you decide upon the people that you want to include in your memoir from any given event, define them by repeating Exercise 17B and Exercise 18A. This will enable you to develop the people that were involved in your life, and thus deepen your memoir.*

Keep moving ahead with the workbook. You still have a number of exercises to do before you understand the essential ingredients of writing memoir.

The Route to Creativity

Back-Work

Back-work is the route to connecting with your

life story; it is the key to writing creatively.

Back-work is the *art* of developing and planning your story. All writing entails back-work. It is a very important element in the creative process. Planning and development are the vital elements that will pay dividends as you write your memoir.

What you are striving to achieve in writing your memoir – which is creative non-fiction – is getting your story on paper in the most creative way possible. The more you develop your story – the more back-work you are willing to do – the more creative your writing will become, and the more you will connect to what you want to write about.

When you start out on any journey, you usually have a destination in mind. This helps you choose the directions and route you are going to take to complete your journey. You know your destination and therefore your direction.

It is exactly the same in writing. Before you start writing your story you must know your destination so that you can carefully plan the direction your journey will take. It is like working backwards so that you can go forward.

In writing you need to know the ending of your story before you begin writing, so that you have a destination. You will then know where you are going, where you will end up, and what route you will take to get there. To arrive at this point requires story development, ie back-work.

You have already started to do back-work on your memoir. From completing all of the previous exercises, you now have a greater understanding of what was going on in your life and the people that were important to you throughout the events, occasions and experiences that you have associated with to date.

You have recalled many memories from your life that were significant to you. All of this back-work will help you define what your memoir will be about. You are not yet ready to fully outline your memoir, but you have started the back-work that will bring you to your destination.

I've met many people in workshops who've started to write stories, both fiction and creative non-fiction, but have then got stuck. They did not know what to do with their story, how to continue, or even what to think about to make it work. This is because they had not done or completed the back-work that was necessary *before* they started to write. They did not know their destination and therefore the direction of their story was hazy, incomplete, and basically all over the place. They were undecided as to which route to follow; they did not understand how to go forward and could not continue with their story.

I do not believe in writing blocks. Writers only fall prey to writer's block when they have not worked out their story before they start to write. In many cases it happens because the writer does not fully understand what they have to *think* about – to solve, to address, to include – to make their story complete.

As mentioned previously, there are rules, elements, guidelines and principles associated with every form of writing – be it journalism, fiction writing, screenplay writing or memoir writing. *Before you can break the rules you have to know the rules.* It is only when you understand these rules that you can truly develop your story.

By completing this workbook you are learning in easy stages the principles of memoir writing – what you have to *think* about in order to creatively complete your memoir.

One of the greatest benefits of back-work is that it makes you develop your story in detail, which in turn enables your writing to flow. Back-work takes the struggle out of writing and allows you to be creative as you write. You will not be sitting for hours thinking about Mr Smith and what he looked like, since you will already have recalled all that you can remember about Mr Smith as you knew him when you were 20 years old.

This is your key to writing creatively. Instead of getting stuck on details and stopping to ask yourself questions about Mr Smith as you are writing, you will be able to creatively describe Mr Smith so that your description is alive and attention-grabbing.

Back-work works!

Note: Understanding and knowing your characters, the events in your life, the culture you belonged to, the environment and the theme of your story allows you to engage creatively with your writing. It will help you to avoid the trap of sitting, thinking and struggling over what to write next.

This is not to say that your memoir will not change direction as you write. It will – but for the better. Your story will take twists and turns that surprise you along the way, routes you were not expecting to travel. You will recall something that you had completely forgotten, incorporating it to enliven your story further. You may even consider a different ending to your memoir. But no matter what you decide to alter and include as you write, it is because you have a direction before you start that permits you to travel forward, unhindered, into the creative process – discovering and enhancing your ability to write creatively.

Your memoir will take surprise twists and turns as you engage with the creative process in your writing journey.

Right-Brain Tip!

By applying the ingredients of back-work to your writing, you cross a creative threshold and uproot a layer of creativity waiting to be explored. It enables you to write from your right brain, using evocative language.

Retracing Your Steps

Summarising

Summarising what you know will tell you

what you don't know.

A Writing Tip!

Sometimes when you bubble you can get lost in bubbles! There are so many thoughts on the page, you are unable to cope with them all. For instance, when you are bubbling about a character, it may seem to you that you have recalled everything about that person. This is the point when you should type or write a full character profile of that person based upon all of your bubbles. You are not writing your story at this stage, just a character profile.

It may surprise you how little you know about them. By doing this exercise you will find out what you *don't* know about the person and what you have left out.

When you finish the character profile, go to a new set of bubbles and recall more memories about that person. Continue doing this, adding to the profile until you are satisfied that you are ready to write about them in your story.

TRUTH

Connecting to Your Path 5

Free Drawing   Exercise 19

Draw what you are feeling right now…with *your left hand.*

Whether you are right-hand dominant or left-hand dominant, use your *left hand* to do this exercise.

Use only chalk or crayons, not pens or pencils.

Use your drawing sketch pad for this exercise.

Remember: try to depict your feelings through symbols and patterns, which means you are using your right brain.

Title and date your work – with your *left hand.*

— research   — events   — ppl
                  — sensory   — evir
                       ex,   — structure

Filing

develop robust timeline
    keep @ front of binder

stop here + organize all
          writings!

The Road to Inspiration

Motivation   **Exercise 20**

Ascertain why you want to write your memoir. This will

encourage you to keep opening your workbook

and to continue writing.

There are many reasons to write memoir. You may want to leave your story to family and friends, or recall an event in your life in order to make sense of it. You may be drawn to this particular genre of writing simply because you feel an affinity with it. Perhaps you have a view to getting your story published, or wish to use memoir as a stepping stone towards finding your writing voice and your inherent ability to create. Maybe you want to use memoir writing as a pathway to exploring your memories, which you may then use to translate your experiences into fiction.

Whatever your motivation, you will definitely learn something and understand more about yourself and your life from writing memoir. It will probably help you to view many events from your life in a different way, and it is very possible that you will find a resolution to significant occasions and events that impacted upon your life. By writing your memoir you will also recall many wonderful events and occasions in your life that you had completely forgotten about.

Exercise A:

1. Sit quietly for a few minutes and think about why and what inspires you to write your memoir.

2. Bubble all your thoughts about why writing your memoir is important to you.

3. When complete, read your bubbles. (You don't have to write a paragraph about it!)

Looking into The Well 2

Including People   **Exercise 21**

Recall the people that were important to you during

various events in your life.

You are beginning to get a picture, an outline of various elements and patterns in your life. You will now develop people in your life further – so that you recall *all* the people that you were associated with during events in your life. Some of the characters you recall you may want to include in your memoir, some you may not. Making those decisions is part of your writing journey and discovering your memoir.

Exercise A:

1. Pick an event or occasion from one of your previous exercises that you want to develop further.

2. In your bubble sketch pad, put the name of that event in a central bubble.

3. Free-associate your thoughts around the following question, using The Bubble Technique:

   • **Who were the *family members* in your life that were around when this event took place?**

4. Start a new bubble and answer the following question:

- **Who were the *friends* in your life that were around when this event took place?**

5. Start another bubble and answer the following question:

- **Who were the *non-relatives* or *non-friends* in your life that were around when this event took place?**

You should name the people as you knew them using titles, nicknames etc, ie Uncle Frank, Mrs Kincaid, Captain Scott, Raggedy Ann etc. Decide which people were really important to the event or occasion.

6. Select these characters one by one and start a new bubble for each person. Recall all you can remember about each person using the questions in Exercise 18A, Part 2 as a guideline.

Remember, when you feel you have recalled all that you can remember about each person, type or write their character profile. This will help you to develop your characters further and show you what you have not included about them. It may also help you to acknowledge how important they are to your story.

This is how you will recall and develop the characters who were significant to each event of your life that you want to include in your overall memoir.

Do this exercise a few times for practice, then move forward in the workbook.

Drinking from The Well 2
Developing People   Exercise 22

Good for future memoirs (handwritten)

Connect with the community you belonged to;

acknowledge the influence it had upon your life.

It is important in memoir writing to associate with the cultures and the communities that you have been a part of so you can show the effect they have had upon your life.

Our personal cultures and communities play a huge part in shaping us. This in turn has a major effect upon how we live, and who in our society we interact with.

Memoir writing is about including not only you the individual, but also the culture and community that you were involved with at a specific time in your life.

For example, think how different your life would be if you lived:

- **in New York City, homeless, on the street**
- **in prison, and in solitary confinement**
- **in a research station at the South Pole**
- **as a missionary in Africa**
- **on a yacht sailing around the world**
- **on an island with 100 inhabitants**
- **in a palace governing a country**

different @ person @ dif stages of life (handwritten)

Can be in many communities @ 1 time (handwritten)

develop each character (handwritten)

I'm not static! (handwritten)

- **in a desert as a nomad**
- **as an astronaut doing research on the moon**
- **in an orphanage or foster care**

How diverse life would be in all of the above situations!

In each instance you would interact differently with your environment and with the community that surrounds you.

Community and culture have different effects upon our lives, depending on *what* community we are a part of and *when* – ie at what point in time we belong to it.

For example: there would be major differences in lifestyle, tradition and values between a 19-year-old African female living in the centre of London, and an African female of the same age living in her tribe in Kenya. There would also be major differences in lifestyle, tradition and values between a 19-year-old living in Kenya in 1930 or a woman of the same age living in Kenya today. In summary: both your community and culture, and their time and era, have profound effects on the values and belief systems that impacted upon your life.

Note: In memoir writing it is important to show community, so that your reader has a greater understanding of your story and the impact that your community had upon your life. You need to weave the events of your life and your community together. This is a vital principle in memoir writing.

Our personal culture is dictated by our:

- **family**
- **career**
- **religion**

- country
- environment
- ethnicity
- traditions
- values

The traditions and background of our culture have a great effect upon us and our belief systems.

A community would include:

The people that were around you – your family group and career will often dictate the people in your community, eg:

- computer technicians
- doctors
- researchers
- single parents
- tribe
- prisoners
- ministers
- orphans
- teachers
- college students
- lawyers

Note: *When you are defining your community at a particular time in your life, think of the people you recall in general terms as a group of people, a type of people, a community of people – not specific people, eg:*

- **an environmental research team**

- a hippie community living with their own social rules
- musicians in a band
- a devout section of religious people in a small neighbourhood
- airline crew
- a black neighbourhood
- a boarding school
- an orphanage
- dancers within a dancing troupe
- a college
- a tribe in central Africa
- an elite group of doctors
- an island community
- sailors within a marina
- lawyers practising at the bar
- soldiers on duty in a foreign country
- cotton farmers in the deep south of the USA
- missionaries in central Africa
- models in Paris in the late 20th century

Your culture will also be defined by:
- the country you lived in
- the location and environment of where you lived ie: urban/country life or city/village
- the ethnicity of your family/people
- the religion you belonged to, if any

It is helpful to ask these questions:

- Were there secrets in your community that had an impact or influence upon your life?
- What were you dealing with in that culture?
- What effect did that culture have upon your life?
- Were there any traditions in your community that defined the way you lived?
- What values did you live by in that culture?

Exercise A:

1. Reread your bubbles from Exercise 21A. In that exercise you developed the people – family members, friends, non-relatives and non-friends – that you were associated with during a particular event in your life.

2. Consider your answers from that exercise and answer the following question:

·What community did you and those people belong to?

Refer to the guidelines above. Maybe there were a few communities involved that subsequently had an influence upon your life.

3. Go to a new page in your bubble sketch pad. Bubble everything you can recall about that community and culture that you were a part of.

4. Concentrate upon the people and the event in that community that you have bubbled about. Recall the significant details of the event. Consider the following questions:

- Who was there?
- Where you were coming from and going to at that

time of your life?
- **What was the person or people doing?**
- **What was your relationship with that person or people?**
- **What did they mean to you?**

Note: *You may feel you have already included all of these answers in your previous questions. Maybe you have, but it is worth continuing. Your answers will surprise you!*

5. Write a new paragraph about the event in Exercise 21A. This time include significant details regarding your community and culture and the people that were in your life at that time. Before you start writing, choose which tense, past or present, you want to write in.

6. Title and date your work.

7. When complete, read your work. Be constructive as you read, noticing whether you stayed within the same tense as you wrote your story.

Note: *This exercise may be done several times, combining different events and people from your life as you weave these occasions with the community and culture that you were involved with at that time. This exercise will provide you with important bedrock material as you write your memoir.*

A Writing Tip!

Reread your writing carefully after this exercise. Be aware of how your writing has developed and how much richer it has become since you started this workbook.

The By-Roads to Freedom

Truth   **Exercise 23**

It is the internal truth of your memoir that remains
unaltered in your writing. The external truth can be altered
– but not to the point where it changes the factual truth.

Truth lies in the by-roads that we don't always want to travel. Yet when we do, we seem to cross a threshold and invite into our lives a new perspective on our past and gain a freedom previously unknown.

I feel it is a huge challenge in our lives to be honest, really *really* honest – and particularly with ourselves. Sometimes we don't even realise we are being dishonest; feelings can get buried and we can live life in denial and refuse to accept the truth. Sometimes withholding the truth can change the course of a life, or lives. Sometimes we cannot cope with the changes honesty will inevitably bring and sometimes it is not the time for the truth to be known.

Truth though is a very elusive part of our lives. We all live in some part with dishonesty – dishonesty with ourselves, dishonesty with our partners, dishonesty with our familes, dishonesty within our working lives.

my truth is dif from Brother's truth... etc. never one real truth

Internal Truth
Internal truth is our personal choice as to how truthful we are with ourselves.

External Truth
External truth is not personal – but it is a large part of our lives.

It seems that at different stages of life individuals confront truth in various ways and with different levels of honesty. For instance, consider how truth would have a different meaning in each of the following circumstances:

- **30-year-old female intent upon excavating her life and being prepared to write about deep trauma from her past**
- **49-year-old living in denial who has always sought comfort from substances**
- **80-year-old recalling the daisies of life, the good times with family and friends and the influences that shaped their lives**

Truth in each of the above situations will vary not only because of age, but because of personal choice and the view of inner and outer worlds. I call this *internal truth*; it is our personal choice as to how truthful we are with ourselves.

External truth is different. It comes from being the observer and relating your view of circumstances.

Think of the following situations where external truth would affect each circumstance:

- **an explorer intent on revealing hidden facets of the world**

• **a journalist reporting from the front line**

• **a doctor being honest with a dying patient**

External truth is not personal, but it is a large part of our lives.

In writing about an event that was significant to you, you will be writing about the effect it had upon you personally. That is your internal truth – your emotional truth about the situation. Another person recounting the same event will have a different slant on it, which will be their internal and emotional truth.

This is what makes us unique as individuals and subsequently what makes our writing unique. What you are always striving for is to be as objective as possible about a situation, to view it with wisdom in hindsight, with no hint of personal judgement or revenge as you recall your experience and tell your truth. Perhaps there is never one real truth in any situation.

Yet it is important to remember that there is a difference between truth and changing the hair colour of the woman who lived next door, or names that you do not want to be made known.

It is the internal truth of your memoir that remains unaltered in your writing. The external truth can be altered, but not to the point where it changes the factual truth.

It is the experience that you are relating in your story which you must stay true to as much as possible. You do not make up experiences in memoir writing. You do not *pretend* things happened – if you pretend, you are writing fiction.

In writing, telling the truth and the enormity of uncovering a life incident can make us vulnerable and hold us back. It can be a blockage point and a great personal challenge, but it can also be a gateway to real freedom.

This challenge often surfaces when one feels incapable of telling the truth about an incident. It is a block that can keep one from writing and creating generally. But it is these charged life incidents that make for good writing. It is our challenge as writers to express these experiences from a distance and without judgement. Ironically, it is the events about which people say, "I couldn't possibly tell that," which usually form the true essence of their stories.

Honesty takes time; time with ourselves and our feelings, time to admit just what was going on, and time to sit with the truth. Dishonest writing comes from holding back on telling the truth, not telling it like it really was.

Our minds are very skilled at finding reasons to avoid the truth, to avoid facing what is really going on within. Sometimes it seems that circumstances will not allow us to be honest, but I feel these are the very circumstances that were sent to challenge us to learn something from. If we take the challenge and transcend the difficulties, what ensues is often life-changing.

Dishonest writing results in one-dimensional work, with little imagery and no impact. Dishonest writing will leave the reader wanting – wanting to know what really happened, wanting to know the truth and ultimately wanting to ditch your story because it is dishonest and hence uninteresting.

Truth is what interests readers and keeps them motivated to continue turning the pages of your story. Honest writing will enliven the realness of your work and draw empathy and understanding from the reader. Honest writing allows the reader to identify with you, the hero or heroine of the story, and the real challenges you faced that shaped your life, which helped shape the person you subsequently became.

Remember, truth in writing has power, not only for you but for the reader. Truthful writing can be recognised instantly.

Honest writing also seems to release us from our pain. It seems that being honest and revisiting a place of trauma or upset allows the gates that were previously closed to reopen. It lifts the taboo. Feelings of inadequacy, fear of rejection and ridicule often stop us from expressing our truth, yet it is only through self-expression that we find the freedom to be who we are.

Writing memoir requires honesty. It requires you to be honest with your story and how you overcame your greatest fears and failures and handled your feats. Writing is a wonderful way to heal your wounds, to touch upon your inner feelings, fears, hopes and desires. Ironically, writing your story honestly will greatly diminish your fears and perhaps set them free forever.

Countless workshop participants have told me that being truthful and revisiting significant events of their lives through writing seemed to unblock trauma for them. It provided a watershed of the event, a freedom they had previously not felt, wonderful memories they had forgotten about, and an ability, mainly because they had revisited forbidden territory in their mind, to translate their story into fiction!

I find this fascinating and I have watched it work. There is something about revisiting the dark places of our lives through memoir writing that allows us to transcend the muddy waters of memory. This in turn provides us with the watershed we are ultimately seeking. It seems it can provide us with bedrock material that ceases to haunt us, and which, with imagination and fantasy, can be transformed into fiction.

There *is* of course fiction in memoir writing, but where do fact and fiction cross over?

There is fiction in memoir writing because it is completely impossible to remember all the details of a particular situation and recount them exactly.

For example, you may remember a particular and very important line of dialogue from a significant event in your life, which is *the* line of dialogue that motivates you to write about that experience; that life-altering sentence that had an impact upon your life and the lives of others.

You most probably will remember where you were when this dialogue was said and who was there, but you may not remember the actual lines of conversation before or after this significant statement took place. You may remember some of it, but you might not remember all of it.

It is the essence of the experience that is all-important. How you choose to fill in the gaps is in part your ability to translate the incident so that the reader will understand it, and most of all, believe you.

A Writing Tip!

It helps if you put yourself into a state of mind of being a self-witness of the event you are trying to write about – as if you are observing your life happening. This allows honesty and truth to become evident in your writing.

You may want to do the following exercises in private and choose to keep them private.

Exercise A:

1. Sit quietly for a few minutes and think about the following question:

- **What was the most honest and difficult conversation you ever had with someone?**

Read the following example:

Title: Being Honest With Dad

I sat at his bedside holding his weathered and bruised hand as I prepared for the doctors to manage this conversation – the big one that he or I had been unable to broach for several years.

This conversation was even more heightened as a forbidden topic given that the sudden deaths of both my mother and brother decades previously had never ever been discussed between us. That was just the way it was and how we coped. It was how we had both learnt to manage our individual losses, and we continued living within this silence.

In that meeting with honesty when the doctor brought up the unmentionable – death – my dad and I were instantly forced to be honest. There was nowhere left to hide, time was running out, we were facing the home run; we were at the cutting edge. This was the time for truth – and we both knew it. It was the moment we both learnt that truth, not silence, was golden.

My dad and I locked eyes when the doctor said that at this stage of his life it was care not cure, and that this would be his final resting place. He then asked us how we had coped with the tragic losses in our lives and what it had meant to us.

I squeezed my dad's hand harder and looked into his big blue and bloodshot eyes, crumbling inside as I watched him crying for the first time in my life. His tears fell hard and fast down his veined and worn cheeks as if the ice pain of loneliness had finally melted.

Suddenly we had broken the silence of death that had existed between us for years. It was one of the most remarkable moments of my life, and I am sure, one of the most remarkable moments in my dad's life too.

With the aid of a wonderful doctor in the hospice we had managed to transcend our blockage point together. It gave us the strength and honesty to discuss life and death in a way we had never been able to do before, and consequently healed a lifetime of wounds between us.

Feeling deeply grateful for all the lessons he had taught me, I watched my dad take his last breath in the world 15 days later, contented and with a smile on his face.

2. Go to your bubble sketch pad. Bubble your thoughts about the most honest conversation in your life.

3. Write a paragraph about it.

4. Title and date your work.

5. When complete, read your work.

Exercise B:

1. Think about all the things in your life *today* you wish you could be honest about, eg:

   • **a particular relationship**

   • **feelings toward another**

   • **family secrets**

   • **sexual preferences**

   • **health**

   • **needs**

   • **hopes**

   • **fears**

   • **a secret relationship**

2. Go to your bubble sketch pad. Bubble about the issues in your life that you would like to be more honest about. Name them.

3. Pick the most significant issue that is affecting your life right now. Choose who you would write to, to tell your situation to. Perhaps a close friend, a doctor, or someone you feel safe confiding in. If the issue involves someone else, perhaps you might choose to write to that person.

4. Write to your chosen person. You don't, of course, have to

send it to them. Tell them honestly what is going on in your life, and how it's affecting you.

5. Title and date your work.

6. When complete, read your work.

Remember, you don't have to show your writings to anyone – these exercises can be kept private.

Exercise C:

1. Think about all the things in your life *in your past* that you wish you had been more honest about.

2. Go to your bubble sketch pad. Bubble about the issues in your life that you would like to have been more honest about. Name them.

3. Pick the most significant issue that you kept quiet about in your past that had an effect upon you.

4. Write another letter revealing this secret to a close friend, or a doctor, or someone you feel safe confiding in. You may even write to someone involved in the secret. Write the letter describing honestly what happened, and how the incident affected you.

5. Title and date your work.

6. When complete, read your work.

Connecting to Your Path 6

Free Drawing   Exercise 24

Draw a wish in your life right now…with your *left hand.*

Whether you are right-hand dominant or left-hand dominant, use your *left hand* to do this exercise.

Use only chalk or crayons, not pens or pencils.

Use your drawing sketch pad for this exercise.

Remember: try to depict your feelings through symbols and patterns, which means you are using your right brain.

Title and date your work – with your *left hand*.

Right-Brain Tip!

This exercise is an example of how Free Drawing can be used at any time as you write, or in between your writings. When you are seeking inspiration with regard to any of your writing concepts, start drawing, using your left hand. Free Drawing helps to free up your thinking patterns and evokes your creativity.

141

Looking Back 2

Congratulations! You have now completed the South East

section of your writing journey.

You have recalled the people and the community that were important and significant to your life, and you have learnt how to merge them with the events, occasions and experiences that were important to you. These are two of the major elements in memoir writing.

You are now well on the writing road. You know which exercises to do to evoke memories about events and people and how to write about them. You can return to these exercises at any stage to develop your thoughts further, but what is important right now is to keep going forward to the next section of your writing journey.

From here you will be expanding upon what you have already learnt, as well as discovering new ways to evoke your creativity that will help you to define your life story further.

Well done! Your writing journey is gaining momentum. It is important to keep moving forward.

A Writing Tip!

Repeat the drawing and sensory exercises that you have already done as often as you can. This evokes your senses and thereby enhances your creativity, enlivening and deepening your writing.

PART 3
Planning Your Journey
Section 3: Environment

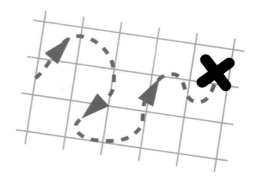

143

The Memoir Map
Environment: WHERE WAS I?

You are now embarking upon the South West
route of your writing journey.

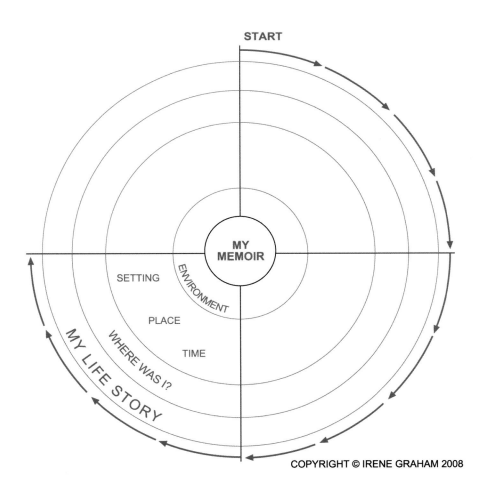

Connecting To Your Path 7

Free Drawing   Exercise 25

Think of your earliest memory. Draw it with your *left hand*.

Our earliest memories often stem from stories we have been told or from photographs that we have referred to throughout our lives. Go back into your well of memory as far as you can and recall your earliest memory.

Whether you are right-hand dominant or left-hand dominant, use your *left hand* to do this exercise.

Use only chalk or crayons, not pens or pencils.

Use your drawing sketch pad for this exercise.

Try to depict your earliest memory using symbols and patterns. This means you are using your right brain.

Title and date your work – with your *left hand.*

Checking Your Compass 6

Sensory Thinking   Exercise 26

Auditory

How often are you aware of the effect that

sound has on you?

In this sensory-thinking exercise explore your auditory sense – your sense of hearing. The buzz of a bee, the scratching of nails on a blackboard, waves breaking against the shore, the shrill whistle of an alarm, a baby crying, a bird singing, children laughing…different sounds evoke varied feelings.

Yet in our everyday lives we forget to stop and listen to the sounds that surround us at every moment. They all have an effect upon us, positive and negative. The sound of silence also has an effect upon us.

Most people recall memories, consciously or unconsciously, when they hear a familiar piece of music. It may remind them of a particular person, time or place. Music can even help you recall an entire conversation.

The exercise below helps you to engage with your ability to listen and to become conscious of what a sound evokes within you. It enhances your auditory sense and strengthens your awareness of the effect sound has upon your feelings.

Exercise A:

1. Select a music track with lyrics, or ask someone to choose a

track for you.

2. Select a new page in your bubble sketch pad.

3. Sit quietly and prepare to listen to the music.

4. Close your eyes to aid deeper concentration. This helps to eliminate outside distractions.

5. Connect to the music as deeply as you can. Be conscious of what it evokes within you. What images come to mind as you listen to the music? How does it make you feel? Happy? Angry? Sad? Content? Uncomfortable?

6. Bubble your thoughts at any stage, either while listening to the music, or when it is finished.

7. When the music is finished, complete the exercise in silence.

8. Write a paragraph. You may write something that was evoked while listening to the music or you may write something apparently unconnected that suddenly comes to mind.

9. Title and date your work.

10. When complete, read your work.

Right-Brain Tip!

Repeat this exercise as often as you like. Even if you are not in a position to write a paragraph each time you hear music, become conscious of it, and ask yourself what feelings the music evokes within you. Become conscious of sounds in your everyday life. Be aware of what they suggest to you.

Looking into The Well 3

Including Environment   Exercise 27

Identify with your environment. Where were you and what was going on around you at the time of your story?

Another important ingredient in developing memoir is to include the environment in which your story takes place. This refers to the setting and the place, as well as the time you are writing about. The details of the environment create atmosphere as you narrate your story using sensory language.

Think of the environment in your story as follows:

• **setting** – the county/region/town/village/street/
                 parish/neighbourhood etc
• **place**   – the actual house/cabin/castle etc
• **time**   – the era/year/season/month/time of day or night

Including details in this way enables the reader to identify with your world and the era you are writing about.

Note: *Naming names in your writing will establish the setting, place and era in your memoir.*

For instance, when I include name details in the following paragraph, notice the difference it makes to the writing content as opposed to omitting the geographical details in the same example in Exercise 17. The changes are highlighted.

Example

Title: Quicksand

*I knew that day, like so many other days, that it was a close call whether I would make the 3pm bus home or not. If I missed this bus it meant waiting an hour for the next one and Mum would be annoyed with me again. I enjoyed being in Karen's **Georgian house** in **South William Street in the centre of Dublin** so much after school that time always went by far too quickly. Her house was so different to mine; there always seemed to be an abundance of people in it, there were so many things to do and the food they ate was not what I ate at home. Her mum was a hairdresser and she let us play in the salon. Karen never made the journey to my house in **Kildare;** it was just too far away. It was another reason, at the ripe age of 10, that I hated living in the country.*

*I ran and ran so that I would make the bus, doing my best to ignore how much my new brown laced shoes hurt. Panting, I looked up **from the top step at Merchant's Arch**, and on the other side of the river crossing **O'Connell Bridge** I saw the **familiar single decker white and red bus**. I figured I could still make it if I ran that bit harder across the **Ha'Penny Bridge,** which was now in front of me. It was a challenge but if the traffic on the other side of the **River Liffey** was slow, which it usually was, I would get to the bus stop before the bus did. As I dashed across the road between cars I encountered a workman's barrier, one of those red and white tape things to keep people out. I ducked under it, and low and behold I was sucked into wet cement, right up my knees, like quicksand. Blushing and humiliated I looked around for help, the bus and my mother's* *annoyance now far from my thoughts.*

Comment

Notice how including names in my story makes the incident become more alive, giving the reader a greater visual representation of the environment.

Including subtle details of the environment in your story contributes to the atmosphere. This allows the reader to identify with a time and place in your life.

Exercise A:

1. Think of a setting you lived in at some stage of your life, one you either liked or disliked.

2. Using your drawing sketch pad, draw this setting, with your *left hand.* **Remember that the setting means the country, region, town, village, street, parish or neighbourhood where you lived. Include as many landmarks as you can, eg forests, shops, buildings, graveyards or any special details you can recall.**

3. In your bubble sketch pad, bubble all the details you can recall about this setting. Name each detail in a separate bubble.

Exercise B:

1. In your drawing sketch pad, draw the place – the actual house, cabin or castle that you lived in at that time with your *left hand.* Include all the rooms, the yard and any buildings connected to the

house. Consider how you would like to depict it; perhaps upright, like a large doll's house, or from an aerial view with the rooms connecting, as an architect would draw.

2. In your bubble sketch pad, bubble the names of each room in the house as you knew them, eg John's room, my room, my mother's sewing room, the garage, the attic, the deck, the porch, the barn etc.

Exercise C:

1. Reread your bubbles from the above exercises regarding the setting and the details of your home.

2. Write a paragraph about living in that house, in the present or past tense. Include names in your story as outlined in the above example.

3. Title and date your work.

4. When complete, read your work.

Drinking from The Well 3

Developing Environment   Exercise 28

Establish the detail in your environment. Absorb the

elements of your surroundings.

There will be times in your writing when it is important to the story to hone in on certain background details that made a difference. At other times, distance is more appropriate, because the details are not important to the story.

Naming household items or objects which were specific to a certain era helps to enhance atmosphere. Examples would be the make and model of a car, or the name of a sweet you remember from your childhood.

Take your time to complete the following exercises, which show you how to establish environment within your memoir.

Exercise A:

1. Refer to your bubbles in A and B of Exercise 27.

2. Start a new bubble in your bubble sketch pad. Bubble about specific memories you have of that home and incidents that happened there, eg:

- **parties**
- **rows**
- **playing games**
- **visitors**
- **Santa arriving**
- **bringing your firstborn home**
- **moving in/moving out**

3. Now pick one of the incidents. Start a new bubble and free-associate around the memories you have about this particular incident. Include as much detail as you can remember.

Exercise B:

1. Think of *the room* this incident took place in. In a new bubble, answer the following questions:

- **What was in the room?**
- **What did the room look like?**
- **What was on the walls?**
- **What sort of floor covering was in the room?**
- **What was the furniture like?**
- **What were the light fittings like?**
- **What were the background sounds or noises?**
- **Was there food in the room?**
- **What type of food was it?**

- Were there flowers in the room?
- What sort of décor did the room have overall?
- What was the dominant colour in the room?
- Was the room cold or hot, musty, clean or dusty?
- Was there a pet or pets in the room?
- Was there a particular fragrance in the room?
- Were there paintings or photographs on the walls?
- What condition was the room in?
- Where were you coming from?
- Where were you going to?
- Name the people in the room.
- Who was doing what?
- What sort of mood were you in?
- What were you feeling?
- What else can you remember about the room, the people, the incident?
- What time of year or season was it?
- What month was it?
- What time of day was it?
- What was the weather like?

2. Reread the paragraph you wrote in Exercise 27C. Then reread your bubbles from the above exercise.

3. Write two or more pages regarding this memory. Include people's names, geographical names and memories about this event. Use close-up detail of the room where the incident took place.

- **Include time details in your story – the era, year, season, time of day etc.**
- **Decide before you write whether you will write in the present or past tense.**
- **Include your retrospective voice in the narrative.**

4. Title and date your work.

5. When complete, read your work.

Well done. You have learnt how to include setting, place and time into your memoir as you recalled a particular incident from your life story.

Note: *To extend this exercise, so that you can include key details of the people that were important to this event, create bubbles for each person as you did in Exercise 18A.*

Merging all three elements together – events, people and environment – enables you to write creative and interesting life stories.

Maintain Your Focus

Action and Synopsis   Exercise 29

The action of your story is shown through events
– under a microscope. The synopsis is the bridge that links
the events together.

When you follow the outline of your back-work, the focus of your life story becomes clearer and helps you decide what you want to include in your memoir, and, as important, what you want to leave out.

Back-work also helps to identify the important events and moments you need to portray in detail. This is the *action* of your story. It comprises the significant details that depict your life story, as if seen through a microscope.

The *synopsis* creates a bridge between the important moments (the action) and the overall details that are less important in your life story.

To understand synopsis and action further, think of yourself as a bird, flying high, looking down, quickly scanning the events and decades in your life. That is the *synopsis.* As the bird flies closer to land it focuses on a particular spot, taking in every detail of that place and time. That is the *action*.

For instance, you may be writing about the time you gave birth to your firstborn. It is the birth that is significant to your story, not the

159

pregnancy. Therefore, the birth is the action that you write and describe in detail, while the nine-month pregnancy is described through synopsis. You move through that nine-month period quickly, but when you get to the time of giving birth, you look through the microscope and write about this stage of your life story in detail.

For example: Synopsis

Writing about your nine-month pregnancy in synopsis could include a page or two describing what your life was like during that time, eg:

> *During that nine-month period I adhered to a very rigid structure in my life, almost to the point of boredom. Each day I walked, ate the right food, rested in the afternoon and went to bed at the same time every night.*

Note: *Even though synopsis is generally brief, it can also include sensory detail with vivid descriptions of how time, you and the people around you evolved through the period in question. Synopsis should be used to strengthen and develop your life story and should include rich details and reminiscences of your life.*

Another example would be writing about the effects that a hurricane had upon your life and your home town. Let's say you were leading a very humdrum life in the months prior to the hurricane, but as soon as the hurricane struck, everything in your life changed – even how you viewed the world thereafter. You might briefly show in synopsis how uneventful your life was prior to the hurricane, and then in the action of the story, recall in detail how everything changed from that moment on.

Example: Action

I did not know if I would survive this hurricane. This was the second natural disaster in my life; I had now lost two homes which felt like two lifetimes had been crushed to dust. Everything was gone. My town was flattened. My grief was deep. My life was in disarray and I did not know where to start to try and rebuild it. I was immobile; it was as if I had turned to stone.

Living in the makeshift shelter increased my fears. I woke every morning and vomited. I could not handle the cries of little children and the sadness in the eyes of the elderly. Sleeping in rows and rows of bodies, stretched out like abandoned corpses, was a far cry from the Egyptian cotton sheets that had adorned my bed in my apartment on 50th Street.

In contrast to synopsis, the action element of your story includes the minute detail of the event in question, ie what was in the room, the actions and reactions of the people involved, dialogue, and your feelings towards the event. The *action* of your story is significant to what your overall story is about. It is the detail of the action that drives your story forward.

The use of action and synopsis in your memoir allows you to develop your memoir so that you do not bore the reader with details that are insignificant and unimportant to your story. This keeps the pace of your memoir moving forward and keeps the reader interested.

The use of action and synopsis is the art of linking your story together.

Exercise A:

1. Refer to the home you lived in, in Exercise 28A. Think of things that often happened in or around that house or things you did many times while living there. Recall a repetitive incident or event covering a span of time with which you associate a lot of memoires, eg:

- **particular parties – at Halloween/birthdays/ Christmas/thanksgiving**
- **recurring visits from a special person**
- **weekly church outings**
- **Friday night music sessions**
- **Grandma's summer visits**
- **bringing a family member to hospital**
- **summer holidays**
- **annual farming responsibilities – sowing corn/bailing hay/picking cotton**

Start a bubble in your bubble sketch pad, naming the overall incidents.

2. Pick one of the incidents. Start a new bubble and free-associate with as many details as you can recall about this recurring episode in your life. Name the people, the things that happened, the time of year, etc.

Study the following example:

Title: Discovery

Summers meant freedom, not only from school but from the 26-mile bus journey that I endured every day of my school life from the age of five. As soon as term finished I became a country kid again, roaming the fields with my dog, discovering life slowly in the countryside, or so it seemed. Like all change I welcomed it with open arms, but as summer progressed I got increasingly frustrated with the lack of action in my life and yearned for the bus journeys that would bring me back to Dublin and my city friends. At the age of 12, just when I felt nothing exciting would ever happen again and that the county was becoming my prison, the doorbell rang, and my world changed forever.

Racing and sliding down our long lino-clad hall ahead of Malcolm, my brother, ducking under his arm to win our frequent door contest, I opened the front door and felt a surge of excitement previously unknown to me. I gazed at the tall guy smiling on the doorstep. His long mop of blonde hair and blue eyes instantly spoke to me. In that moment I discovered boys. Ian, my brother's best friend from boarding school had not only arrived unexpectedly to our home, but had arrived unexpectedly in my life and brought with it a new level of excitement. Suddenly, summer was back, and I was ready to explore a whole new mystery.

This is a very brief example of synopsis and action. The synopsis recalled summers in my life in general, which then evolved into a particular incident one summer which marked a turning point in my life. Notice the close-up detail in the second paragraph as I described how Ian entered my life.

3. Write two or more pages in synopsis about the recurring episode in your life that you bubbled about. Allow it to evolve into an action that was significant to your memories.

4. Title and date your work.

5. When complete, read your work.

A Writing Tip!

Be aware of *action* and *synopsis* within memoir. When reading memoirs, be conscious of how authors handle this element of writing.

Asking for Directions

Research

Research is the key to filling in the missing pieces that are

inherently important to your story.

There are possibly many facts and details of your life that you feel unsure of but want to include in your memoir. Research is the key.

With access to the internet, the scope of information now available is vast. It is important that the facts within your story – dates, street names, names of buildings etc – are correct. It is annoying to a reader for the author to state something factual that is not true and correct. It shows you did not care enough to get it right, and this lowers the authoritative voice in your memoir.

There is also the element of personally exploring family factors and including this understanding in the writing of your memoir.

There are several ways to generate research. It is almost like taking on the persona of a detective to see what you can uncover, in order to gain clarity about a situation and understand it further.

Research will enhance your writing. The closer you get to the facts of your story, the deeper and more informative your writing will become.

Research Examples:

• Gather old photographs, journals, letters etc, both from your life and the lives of others amongst your family and circle of friends who are important to your story.

• Research the people you want to write about, living or not. If they passed on in an era you know nothing about, research that period in history to understand the time they lived in.

• Interview the people you want to include in your memoir. Ask them for their opinion on a subject matter or relative. Get them to tell you their point of view on a given subject you are writing about.

• Visit old houses and towns that are important to your memoir. It is amazing what you will discover and how a sense of place enlivens your writing.

• Look up old relatives and friends of your family and interview them as though you are a journalist. Make a list of the questions you want answers to before you meet them.

• If you are writing about a war, research that war, become familiar with the events and what happened so that you can write about it informatively. Do this for each *subject* matter that you are including in your memoir.

• Read old newspaper cuttings from the era you are writing about. This will help you understand the society and the time in question.

• If your memoir includes an illness, research the facts behind that illness so that you understand it in depth.

• Visit libraries and research books written about the period

or topic you are writing about.

· **Look up genealogy records of your family.**

Note: *It is important not to get so bogged down in research that you feel incapable of writing your story.*

A Writing Tip!

Research brings a deeper vision to your story. Through it you will find things you were not even searching for! Research also gives you the impetus to write.

A Writing Tip!

Use a recording device to record interviews. Keep it with you to record ideas and notes for yourself as you research and think about your memoir.

Connecting to Your Path 8

Free Drawing   Exercise 30

Draw anything with your *left hand.*

Whether you are right-hand dominant or left-hand dominant, use your *left hand* to do this exercise.

Use only chalk or crayons, not pens or pencils.

Use your drawing sketch pad for this exercise.

Draw anything; do not pre-decide what it is you are going to draw.

Let your *left hand* guide you, follow it, and see what happens.

Connect to what you are drawing and ask yourself what it means to you. As you draw, think of a title for your work.

Title and date your work – with your *left hand.*

Looking Back 3

Congratulations! You have now completed the South West

section of your writing journey.

You have recalled many events and people that were important in your life. You know how to incorporate them into places and settings.

You have traversed a significant part of your journey. You have not quite completed your writing journey, but you are definitely making fast progress and moving in the right direction.

Keep moving forward, there is more fun ahead. You will learn how to bind your work together and to *think* like a writer.

Well done! You have learnt a vast amount about writing your memoir. It is important to keep moving forward.

A Writing Tip!

Keep referring to your Time Lines and bubbles. Start looking for patterns in your life – this helps you to recognise how to focus your memoir.

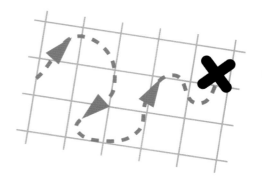

The Memoir Map

Structure: HOW DO I OUTLINE MY MEMOIR?

You are now embarking upon the North West

route of your writing journey.

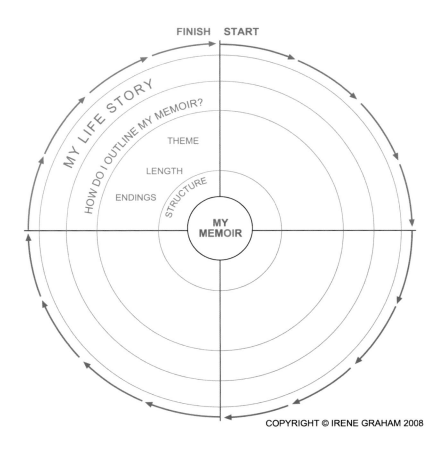

Checking Your Compass 7

Sensory Combining   Exercise 31

Sensory combining is a powerful way to integrate

and deepen sensory awareness.

This is a fun exercise and one that workshop participants *always* say is impossible – until they are amazed by the final paragraph they write.

Applying the same guidelines as in the previous sensory-thinking exercises, complete the following exercises. It is even more fun if you do them with someone.

Note: It is important to read and complete these exercises one by one, one step at a time. Exercise A, then Exercise B, then Exercise C, then Exercise D. Do not jump ahead. Do not read what the next exercise is or it will not have the same impact. This is important. This is a powerful exercise that enhances creative writing. Complete it as instructed.

To get started, select the following:

A. A food product you want to taste. For best effects make sure it is sweet, sour, bitter or salt flavoured. Select a different item than used previously.

B. *A* music track with lyrics, (different to the one used previously).

C. A photo from your family album (also different to the one used previously).

You are now ready to start the exercises.

EXERCISE A: *Taste*

1. Close your eyes.

2. Taste the food item.

3. Bubble your thoughts.

4. In *seven* minutes, write a paragraph on what the food item evokes within you.

5. Title and date your work.

EXERCISE B: *Auditory*

1. Sit quietly and prepare to listen to the music.

2. Start the music.

3. Close your eyes. Connect to the music as deeply as you can. How does the music and the lyrics make you feel?

4. When you are ready, bubble your thoughts in a new bubble.

5. In *seven* minutes, write a paragraph on what the music evokes within you.

6. Title and date your work.

EXERCISE C: *Visual*

1. Study the photograph. What memories does it evoke for you?

2. Bubble your memories in a new bubble.

3. In *seven* minutes, write a paragraph on what the photograph evokes within you.

4. Title and date your work.

EXERCISE D:

1. Reread what you wrote in the last three exercises.

2. In *ten* minutes, write a new paragraph – rephrasing your writing and linking the above three paragraphs together. This is possible! Your link may be a word, a person, a theme, a place or anything – try it, and see what happens.

3. Title and date your work.

4. When complete, read your writing from all the exercises.

> **A Writing Tip!**
>
> You now understand how sensory thinking works. You can do this exercise on an ongoing basis using different combinations of sensory triggers for your writing. It is a powerful exercise to deepen thinking, enhance creativity and strengthen your writing voice.

The Purpose of Your Journey

Theme   Exercise 32

Theme is the purpose of your journey, the message of
your story – the hook that binds your work together.

Every story has a message. Your life story will be far more interesting if you find the message – the hook upon which to focus your memoir.

To bind your work together you need to find the *theme* of your memoir. Theme is more often implied than stated. It provides the direction of your story and focuses your work. Theme allows your writing to find a form, remain interesting to the reader, and relate the message you want to tell in the best way possible. Staying aware of your theme helps avoid going off on a tangent writing about incidents that do not relate to your overall story.

The Time Line of your life that you started in this workbook will help you greatly here – if you do it honestly, and spend as much time as you need. It may take days or weeks, but what you discover from taking time and recalling your life in this way is very significant. Your Time Line will not only help identify the theme of your story, but will highlight subject matters to base your memoir on. It shows you what has motivated or affected you throughout your life; for example people, your career, your religion, an illness, circumstances, or even being in a place at the right or wrong time.

It is important to remember that your life story may involve a number of subject matters that relate to different themes. It requires careful consideration as to which subject matter and what theme you want to focus your memoir on. And you might have several memoirs to write. Your memoir may also consist of one long story or it may involve several short stories. Either way, your writing and subject matter should be focused around theme.

For instance: the life of one of my workshop participants was very affected by a childhood illness of her younger sister. She wrote beautifully about various incidents with this sister. She touched upon the essence of what it took not only for her parents, but for her, and the other members of her family, to develop the best life that was possible for this little girl. She related how as a child, teenager and adult she felt guilty and anxious when her sister was away from home in special care – which granted the competence essential for her development.

Throughout the workshop, the participant wrote of many incidents that affected her due to these separations. The more she wrote, the guiltier she felt. I realised the theme of her stories; *sometimes you have to be cruel to be kind.*

Naming the essence of her story in this way allowed this writer to focus her memories, and motivated her to explore in depth what the separations from her sister meant. The times she went on vacation without her. The Christmases that were challenging without her, and the family occasions her sister missed out on. Naming the theme helped the writer to recall the family's physical home, and how it had to be different to accommodate for her sister's needs. Identifying with the theme enabled the writer to depict the strength of the family, and what the illness took from and gave to the lives of these people.

The theme also allowed the author to discard the inclination to write about other incidents that had no significance to her story. It allowed the writer to revisit memories of how the situation with her sister subsequently affected *her* life – which strengthened her writing and deepened her story.

In memoir writing you are seeking to isolate the *subject* of your life story, and then connect that subject matter to a theme. Refer to the various subject matters and themes in the following examples:

Subject: **Materialistic fortune**

Theme: *Money can't buy happiness.*

This memoir might be centred upon the life of a child and adult who was fortunate materialistically but who never found love with parents or partners. It might be the story of the author's journey through life and what he or she had encountered because of money, what had subsequently been lost because of money – and what was ultimately gained because of these experiences.

Subject: **A crazy family**

Theme: *It takes all sorts to make the world.*

This memoir could be about a 'crazy' family, their inter-relationships and how they managed to overcome or not their addictions, abuse experiences and episodes into crime, explaining the effect it all had.

Subject: **A travel memoir**

Theme: ***One half of the world does not know how the other half lives.***

This could be the theme for a travel memoir. The author could relate the experiences of their travels into little known territories and how those experiences not only affected their life, but what they learnt as a result of interacting with other parts of the world.

Subject: **An inspirational person**

Theme: ***All good things must come to an end.***

This theme might relate to the life of an author and how a parent or person had inspired them, and the subsequent effect this person had upon their life, even after their death.

Subject: **Religion**

Theme: ***Different strokes for different folks.***

This theme might show how religion affected the author's young life and the challenge and changes it subsequently brought to the family unit in adult life because of different beliefs.

Subject: **A war veteran**

Theme: ***Life isn't all beer and skittles.***

This theme might relate to the life of a young war

veteran, the experiences of interacting with another culture during the war, and the subsequent effects war had upon his or her life.

What is common I feel, and quite extraordinary, is that theme concepts in memoir writing seem to relate to the underlining *feelings* of the author – your attitude towards the subject. Thus your *feelings* regarding the subject will alter how you relate your story, how you approach it, and what you write about.

For instance, the theme associated with the above war veteran memoir would alter dramatically if the writer decided to base their story upon forming a relationship with a man or woman in enemy territory – as opposed to the effects that joining the army had on their life. Both stories may include this relationship, but the chosen theme will alter the memoir significantly, eg:

Subject: **A war veteran**

Theme 1: *Life isn't all beer and skittles.*

Theme 2: *Love will find a way.*

Therefore, depending upon the implied theme, the *feelings* of the author towards the subject matter will alter how the writer relates his or her experience of being a war veteran.

Identifying with the theme of your subject deepens the meaning of your memoir.

Theme is a fascinating part of the writing jigsaw. It demands thought and insight from the writer, and a personal investigation on a deeper level as to what it is you want to communicate. If you are honest and connect to the basic feelings around the path your life has taken, you will probably more easily be able to connect to the theme most appropriate for your memoir.

Do not get discouraged if you cannot put your theme into words immediately. Sometimes you will come upon the theme for your story instantly, but sometimes it takes longer to clarify what it is you want to say, and that's OK.

The following exercises help you define the *theme* of your life story. Take your time while doing these exercises. Contemplate your answers – you will learn a lot about your personal life journey.

Exercise A:

1. Think of various times in your life when you experienced any or all of the following feelings:

- **fear**
- **joy**
- **grief**
- **amusement**
- **hope**

2. Take a new bubble for each feeling. Free-associate about the times and events that made you feel this way. Name the events. You do not have to go into detail about them at this stage.

Exercise B:

1. What has affected you most in your life? Reflect upon the following questions:

- **unrequited love?**
- **abandonment?**
- **death and loss of loved ones?**
- **displacement from your country of origin?**
- **abuse?**
- **addiction?**
- **bullying?**
- **effects of natural disasters?**
- **political life?**
- **crime?**
- **betrayal?**
- **materialistic circumstances?**
- **travel?**
- **foster care or adoption?**
- **war?**
- **religion?**
- **illness?**
- **parent-child relationships?**
- **husband-wife relationships?**
- **sibling relationships?**
- **exploitation?**
- **exile?**

2. Take a new page in your bubble sketch pad. Bubble about experiences in your life that have had an effect upon you based upon the above list and include anything else that affected your life. You do not have to go into detail at this stage.

Exercise C:

1. In your bubble sketch pad, bubble your answers in detail to the following question, based upon your answers in the above question:

- **What has affected you most in life?**

Exercise D:

1. Consider the following:
- **What do you know most about?**
- **What do you feel strongly about?**
- **What has inspired you in your life?**
- **What are you passionate about?**
- **Do you have a repetitive dream in your life?**
- **What haunts you?**
- **What times in your life have you felt defeated?**
- **What do you think about a lot?**
- **What positive areas of your life do you repeat over and over?**
- **What negative things in your life do you repeat over and over?**

2. Make a new central bubble in your bubble sketch pad for each of the above questions. Free-associate with your thoughts as you bubble your answers.

Exercise E:

Focus upon different stages of your life. Look at the various decades of your life and name them.

Example:

0 to 10   – Lived in the country. Moved home a lot.

10 to 20   – Discovered my independence. Left home for the city. Started to write.

20 to 30   – Fell in love. Went wild. Travelled a lot. Wrote a lot.

And so on.

1. Draw each decade of your life on a Time Line. Focus on what was most prevalent in your life through each decade. Focus on significant years in your life. Name them, eg: the year…

   • **I found out I was adopted**
   • **I left home**
   • **I moved continents**

Exercise F:

1. Reread all your work from the above exercises. Answer the following questions:

   • **What topics or patterns keep emerging in your life?**
   • **How might you focus a memoir around these elements of your life?**

Think about possible *subject matters* for your memoir with regard to your life story, eg:

   • **injustice**
   • **being adopted**
   • **life behind bars**

- **growing up black in a white neighbourhood**
- **addiction**
- **travel**
- **specific family location that affected generations**
- **extreme religious beliefs**
- **a particular illness**

2. Select personal topics from your work and place them in a central bubble. Make a new bubble for each topic. Free-associate your thoughts around each topic, see what comes up. Do not judge your answers or limit what you write on the page.

Exercise G:

1. When you find a topic or subject matter from your life that really ignites how you think, and unites the essence of who you feel you are as a person – keep free-associating with this topic until you can *name* your theme, eg *different strokes for different folks.*

> **A Writing Tip!**
>
> Keep these questions in your head. Refer to them often. Think about them as you go about your daily life. Watch your thoughts. Your answers to these questions will unearth your subject matter and the theme of your memoir.

Connecting to Your Path 9

Free Drawing   Exercise 33

Draw what you are feeling right now...with your *left hand.*

Whether you are right-hand dominant or left-hand dominant, use your *left hand* to do this exercise.

Use only chalk or crayons, not pens or pencils.

Use your drawing sketch pad for this exercise.

Remember: try to depict your feelings through symbols and patterns, which means you are using your right brain.

Title and date your work – with your *left hand.*

A Writing Tip!

Check your finished drawing. Does it relate to the theme of your memoir? Your drawing may provide another clue to the message of your memoir.

Choosing Your Pace

The Art of Time

Establishing the present and going back and moving

forward in time within your memoir -

this is the art of time.

Time is another important element in the memoir mix which helps you to creatively outline and structure your memoir. Memoir does not need to be written chronologically, and is far more interesting when it is not.

Consider how time is portrayed in movies. *A flashback* scene tells the audience of an important element in the story that happened in the past. In order to establish the past, the viewer will have already related to the time in the present in which the character is living.

The process is similar in memoir writing. You decide which point in time from your life story you want your memoir to be set in. This point of reference establishes the *present* time of your story.

By establishing this, you can go back in time, you can go further back in time, and you can go forward in time, as you relate your story. Thus, you need to be explicit as to what point in your life is the present time of your story. This provides clarity in your writing as your life story unfolds.

By creating the present you allow time to become focused. This enables you to guide your story back and forth as you set up a time frame that the reader can easily relate to. This also allows you to structure your thoughts with regard to time.

The present in your story will work better if it holds conflict, struggle and drama. This will immediately catch the reader's attention, providing a platform to show the reader how you got to this point – and how that event affected your life, before and after, this time.

The present does not need to be today. It can be any point in time within your life story that you choose to establish as the now.

The *present* is your centre, your axis – the heart of your story.

For any memoir, you need to decide where your story begins. You need to draw upon a poignant time that will immediately capture the reader's attention.

For example, in a book about the experience of exile, the subsequent struggle to gain citizenship in a foreign country, and how it all affected your life, the start of your story could be:

• **The day you sat awaiting your fate in the immigration office, waiting for your number to be called.**

• **The moment you climbed into a makeshift boat to leave your country.**

• **The morning you dressed for the ceremony to swear allegiance to your new country.**

From this point you can move around in time by

including sentences such as:

- • nine months later…
- • the following day…
- • earlier that month…
- • later that same year…
- • a decade later…
- • two weeks after that…
- • that was a long time ago now…

By establishing the now, the reader will understand that you are either reminiscing about the past or looking forwards into the future as you narrate your memoir.

As you write your memoir, it is important to use the *present* established within your story as a reference point, from which to move back and forth.

Note: *The time element in your memoir is also related to the structure of your story, which is defined further in the chapter on structure.*

Are We Nearly There?

Story Length

> *How long should your story be?*
>
> *The answer is, there is no answer!*

There are no set rules for how long your memoir should be. Your story will be the length that you want it to be, or will be as long as it takes to tell your story.

Stories vary from a couple of pages to the size of a full length book. You may choose to write your memoir by telling a series of short stories, or you may write it as one long story.

When you complete all the development and back-work for your story, you will have a sense as to how long your memoir will be. Then as you subsequently follow your path and go forward with your planned directions, you will arrive at your destination – the ending of your story.

Hooray! We're Here!

Story Endings

When you complete the back-work for your memoir you know where you want your story to end. But it is through the creative act of writing that you find the actual conclusion to your memoir.

As you continue your writing journey and write your memoir, you will know the direction that your story will take and therefore where you are heading – the destination, the ending of your story. You will know where you are going so that you can keep your story on track, tying it to your theme as you move forward with your writing.

Endings in memoir writing encompass many patterns. It is not like writing a story of fiction where you can neatly tie all the elements together to make it complete. Real life is not like that.

The destination of your memoir will be a specific point in your life that completes the memoir you have chosen to write. How you actually narrate the ending to your memoir becomes clearer to you as you engage with the creative process of writing.

You may consider using the following pointers to end your memoir:

- a retrospective voice narrating events you previously visited in your story and what they mean to you today

- ending with a question that only time will give you an answer to

- looking forward, having found an answer to a question that you raised throughout your memoir

Whatever route you take to complete your memoir, your story should conclude naturally in a way that satisfies you and your readers.

Arranging Your Journey

Structure

How you mix the ingredients of your life story provides the structure to your memoir.

How you choose to arrange and structure your personal story is a large part of the creative process and encompasses all of the aspects of memoir writing that you have learnt to date.

Structuring of your story is about deciding how to put the pieces of your jigsaw together. It is about choosing how to bind all of your chosen ingredients so that your story remains focused and interesting and allows you to capture and retain the reader's attention.

What is the best way to construct your memoir?

Consider the following questions:

- **What is the best tense to write my story in – past or present?**
- **What time period works for my story?**
    - –a day?
    - –a week?
    - –a month?
    - –a year?
    - –a decade?
- **At what point should I start my story so that I immediately capture the reader's attention?**

- Should I tell it as one long story or as several short stories?
- How should I focus the chapters of my story? What headings would be appropriate? Should I use
    - dates?
    - locations?
    - people?
    - events?

All of these questions are personal choices by the author and define individual creativity in storytelling. It is important to know the answers to these questions before you write your memoir. Become aware of authors' choices and how they choose to define and construct their memoirs.

All stories require structure – a beginning, a middle and an end. It is important to define where you want to start your memoir, where it will bring you to, and how you will end it.

In the next section of the workbook you will learn how to visually map your story so that you follow your direction and destination with ease.

A Writing Tip!

To help structure your memoir, divide it into three sections – a beginning, a middle and an end. Use the following principle as a basic guideline to gauge the length of each section of your overall story:

Beginning – one quarter

Middle   – one half

End   – one quarter

Right-Brain Tip!

Refer to The Memoir Map often. Use it as a visual image to uncover your memoir.

A Writing Tip!

Defining the outline and structure of your memoir before you write your life story allows you to engage in the creative process on a deeper level. It also provides greater writing enjoyment.

Connecting to Your Path 10

Free Drawing   Exercise 34

Draw anything with your *left hand.*

Whether you are right-hand dominant or left-hand dominant, use your *left hand* to do this exercise.

Use only chalk or crayons, not pens or pencils.

Use your drawing sketch pad for this exercise.

Draw anything.

Do not pre-decide what it is you are going to draw. Let your *left hand* guide you, follow it, and see what happens.

Connect to what you are drawing and ask yourself what it means to you. As you draw, think of a title for your work.

Title and date your work – with your *left hand.*

Looking Back 4

Congratulations! You have completed the North West

section of your writing journey.

You have also completed The Memoir Map and the four elements of your writing journey:

- **events**
- **people**
- **environment**
- **structure**

You traversed the high roads and by-roads of your personal life journey. You have a greater understanding of your life story and have enhanced your writing voice.

You have a clearer vision of how to write your memoir, how to focus it, and what you have to develop further to make it work. You understand the need for back-work and what you have to think about before you start your book.

You can navigate the remainder of your journey with confidence as you learn how to tie the knots and bind all of the ingredients together.

Well done! Enjoy the remainder of your writing journey as you travel towards your destination.

PART 4
Navigating With Confidence

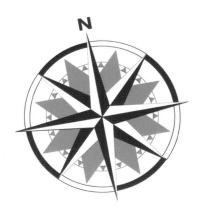

COPYRIGHT © IRENE GRAHAM 1994

Reversing

The Delete Button

Do not be afraid to scratch things out when

bubbling or writing.

As mentioned previously, I do not believe in writing blocks. When you are engaged in writing and suddenly you stop, that is the time to go back over your work, to reverse, and to move your thoughts in a different direction.

Remember the writing trick from the chapter 'Signposts', Exercise 3 – to scratch out the last bubble or the last two or three bubbles so that your thoughts can move forward in a different direction. Also apply this method to your writing.

A Writing Trick!

When you are writing and suddenly you stop, as if the creative flow momentarily dries up, scratch out the last sentence, or the last two sentences or even the last three sentences. Reread your previous sentences or paragraph and continue writing.

Advanced Mapping

Combining Your Knowledge

Advanced mapping enables you to

see your story.

As your story develops it is important to be able to *see* it, so that you can plan each stage of your story. Advanced mapping allows you to do this.

The Time Line you developed in Exercise 10 will help you to plan your life story, and to work out the overall structure of your memoir.

What you need to envision is a beginning, a middle and an end to your story – and where your starting point will be.

Since you have completed the exercises in this workbook one by one and recalled many memories, events, people and places from your life story, you are now in a position to answer the following questions.

There are six basic questions that you need to answer before you start writing your memoir.
1. **What is the subject of my story?**
2. **What is the theme of my story?**
3. **How will I write my story?**
4. **What is the structure of my story?**
5. **What is the outline of my story?**

6. What is the time period of my story?

For example:

Let's look at a hypothetical memoir based upon the life of a war veteran. I chose this topic because it is current and possibly something everyone can relate to. It is an example only of how the Time Line can be used to plan and plot a memoir.

Let's say I am a 23-year-old male war veteran and I want to write my memoir based around the war, my life prior to the war and why I enlisted. I also want to portray the effects war had upon me and the challenges war subsequently brought to my life.

Based upon the six questions, I have defined the story as follows:

1. What is the subject of my story?

   — my life as a war veteran

2. What is the theme of my story?

   — life isn't all beer and skittles

3. How will I write my story?

   — in the first person, past tense

4. What is the structure of my story?

   — each chapter will define the challenges of war, based upon various aspects of my experience. I will also incorporate flashbacks and use the retrospective voice, between sentences, to highlight my personal struggles.

5. What is the outline of my story?

   — each *chapter* is topic-driven as I narrate my war

experiences, eg:

— killing a person at close range

— becoming friends with a woman enemy

— fighting with my mates

— tank claustrophobia

— paranoid effects upon returning home

6. What is the time period of my story?

— the memoir is set over a 28-day-period throughout my lecture tour to students in different locations

Study the following two Time Lines:

• Time Line 1: *Overall* Chapter Content

• Time Line 2: *Final* Chapter Content

Note: *A Time Line for your memoir can be any length. These are brief examples and not complete with regard to the above story.*

TIME LINE 1: *Overall* Chapter Content

Beginning

- my first lecture; a shocking question posed by a student

-

- getting hit by a bullet

-

- getting to know a woman from enemy territory

Middle

- my first bomb

-

- killing a person at close range
- fighting with my mates
- tank claustrophobia

-

- leaving the war, my mates and the woman I came to respect

End

- arriving home – Christmas with Mum

-

- paranoid behaviour

-

- my final lecture; reminiscences from my life story

TIME LINE 2: *Final* Chapter Content
Chapter: Reminiscences from my life story

Beginning

-
-
- shooting ball with friends
- remembering playing with guns as a kid
-
- asking Smithy to run away to the army with me
-
- admitting to my mum that I had joined the army

Middle

-
-
-
- getting fit
-
-
-
- understanding more of the enemy

End

-
- how I feel now
-
-
- what I want now
-
- what the future holds

Defining your story in this way helps to:

- move details around and judge what works
- judge what is important and what is not important
- switch chapter positions
- delete/add information
- revise the structure

In three stages construct your memoir as follows:

a) Initially, you must answer the six basic questions outlined at the beginning of this chapter.

b) When you have answered these questions, define each chapter, constructing it on a Time Line, for the *overall* story as highlighted above.

c) Use a new Time Line for *each* chapter to define the chapter content, as highlighted above.

Remember: a beginning, a middle and an end for each chapter helps move your story forward. It keeps it interesting and highlights what to include and what to leave out. This allows you to focus upon the important details of your life, the characters you want to include and the finer points of your experiences that will enliven your story.

Note: Personalise ways to use a Time Line for your life story. Use it to work out the structure of your memoir – play with time, order, rework and revise the outline for the chapter details. This is a very accurate way to see your story before you start your book. It will become apparent to you when you have discovered the plot of your story – you will see it working on the Time Line.

A Writing Tip!

Fill in the chapters and content of each chapter on your Time Lines with the information you know. You do not have to wait until you know *all* the answers, you can skip backwards and forwards. *Seeing* your writing represented in this way helps you to discern what you have to include, and what you can exclude.

Right-Brain Tip!

Using Time Lines in this way before you start writing your book provides you with your direction and your destination. It allows you to write creatively without stopping and starting, wondering what to write next or questioning who you are writing about. The use of this method allows you to stay in your right brain and write creatively – because you have a visual image of your story.

The Right Track

Evocative Language   Exercise 35

Evocative language comes from the heart and helps the

writer to express emotion.

As discussion on evocative and figurative language could entail a whole book in itself, it is not the purpose here to define it fully, but rather to make you aware of its existence. As you develop your unique writing voice and your personal style of writing, remember to incorporate evocative language into your work.

Evocative language comes from the heart; it allows for expression and connection to our experiences. It is achieved by using figurative language – through the use of metaphors, similes, imagery, alliteration and symbolism, which are but a few classifications within figurative language.

Figurative language is not literal language; it is language that has a deeper meaning than what it is saying on the surface.

In brain research, it is noted that evocative language is characteristically right-brain language. It uses imagery, sensory details and is rich in associations. It involves our emotions. Objective, descriptive language is characteristically left-brain language. It is accurate and clear, and has precise meaning. Studies on this subject matter are still relatively new and ongoing in the world of brain research.

Left-brain language is precise language; it is used in documents to define exactly what is being stated. Legal documents use precise language.

Right-brain language is evocative language, often used in poetry. It is suggestive and filled with sensory details that connect to our emotions. Evocative language uses connotative words to imply suggestion in addition to the literal meaning. It also uses associative words which form a mental connection between ideas and relationship. Writing creatively employs the use of evocative language, without overusing it.

Example:

Title: Easter Eggs

*The black and white TV used to enthral us to a state of near hypnotism **like medicated patients in an institution**. It was a regular fight as to who would put the kettle on for supper. That particular Sunday, I didn't mind. I could secretly nibble a piece of chocolate and forgo the game of who could keep their Easter eggs the longest. It was a good Easter that year; my brother, sister and I received 36 eggs in total – **a mountain of ecstasy** arranged neatly on the sideboard in the kitchen.*

*I crossed the **dimly lit hall**, automatically opening the door an inch to flip the light switch and keep Patsy and Peggy, my cocker spaniels, at bay. Eager to rejoice over my stash of chocolate, the absence of their usual trick of trying to **bounce out the door** went unnoticed. Then shock, horror and utter devastation suddenly ripped through my world. Silver paper and cardboard covered the kitchen floor. There* *wasn't a scrap of chocolate in sight as my identical twin dogs lay* **amidst the carnage and added another day to my annual state of abstinence.**

Study the highlighted sentences in the above example and note the use of figurative language:

simile – like medicated patients in an institution

metaphor – a mountain of ecstasy

imagery – dimly lit hall / bounce out the door

alliteration – amidst the carnage and added another day to my annual state of abstinence

Note: Notice how figurative language creates deeper meaning and enhances writing creatively. As you become familiar with your writing voice and the use of sensory detail and figurative language, you will find a deeper expression in your writing.

Exercise A:

1. Reread your bubbles from Exercise 28A, Part 3, where you bubbled about a specific incident that took place in a particular room in your home.

2. Write a paragraph about this particular *room.* Include sensory detail, imagery, and perhaps a simile or some form of figurative language to enhance your writing.

3. Title and date your work.

4. When complete, read your work.

A Writing Tip!

It is important in writing creatively that you do not overwrite your work, creating long and complex sentences bursting with figurative language. This makes your writing contrived and the reader will soon lose interest.

Turning The Key

Story Entry Point

It is the way into *your memoir that is all important – your personal key and route to recalling an experience.*

You now know how to tap into your experiences and evoke memories so that you can write about them creatively. You are most likely able to identify which exercises evoke your creativity, and which exercises are not so easy for you. Remember: work with both. In this way you develop your ability to work with both sides of your brain.

The key to tuning into your personal memoir is based upon one of the following routes:

> **events** might evoke and recall substantial details **or**

> **people** might trigger significant memories **or**

> **places** may provide easier access.

Find your key. Know which route is the easiest for you. Events, people or places trigger memories of your experiences.

Remember it is the way *into* your memoir that is important – your personal key and route to recalling an experience. Whichever way you find easiest is the way into your memories, *for you.*

Ask yourself the following questions, based upon what you have already written to date:

• Which *event* in my life meant the most to me when I recalled it on my Time Line?

• Which *person or people* resonated with me when I developed people in my life?

• What *community* shaped my life the most?

• What *location or setting* had a significant impact upon my life when I recollected past environments?

Keep this in mind. Ask yourself the above questions. See what route you connect to. As you think about or reread the work you have developed to date, the answers will resonate with you.

How one recollects experiences and memories is totally individual and different for each person.

A Writing Tip!

Develop your memoir using your chosen route. Then flip back and forth along the other two routes to develop your memoir further. Always start with bubbles. This is how you build upon your journey and find experiences that you want to write about.

Remember: memoir writing consists of all three routes. You have to include each one – but start with the route that is easiest for you.

Connecting to Your Path 11

Free Drawing   Exercise 36

Draw what you are feeling right now…with your *left hand.*

Whether you are right-hand dominant or left-hand dominant, use your *left hand* to do this exercise.

Use only chalk or crayons, not pens or pencils.

Use your drawing sketch pad for this exercise.

Remember: try to depict your feelings through symbols and patterns, which means you are using your right brain.

Title and date your work – with your *left hand.*

Where Are You?

The Route Forward

You have travelled a long way since you did your first exercise.

Now for fun, and for feedback, compare your drawings from Exercise 2 and Exercise 36 'Connecting to Your Path 2' and 'Connecting to Your Path 11'.

The first exercise you did with your *right hand* (if you are right hand dominant) – the last exercise you did with your *left hand*.

Note what has happened in your drawings:
- **Are they bigger on the page?**
- **Are they more definite?**
- **Do they say more to you?**
- **Are the colours bolder?**
- **Do you feel you have discovered something by comparing them?**
- **Are there any similarities between the two?**
- **Are the titles similar or different?**

Think about what both drawings mean to you and the overall process of what you feel you have achieved. What would you like to achieve now in your writing?

Seeing Forward

Congratulations ! ! ! ! ! ! !

The Memoir Writing Workbook *is now complete.*

Take a bow!

You focused upon your life story and recalled your memories – now you know how to structure and write your memoir. You have developed many ways to tap into your imagination and write creatively.

You have written many pieces about your life – who was important to you, where you were and how events shaped who you have become. You developed your unique writing voice and discovered how to enhance it as you incorporated your thoughts into your memoir using your retrospective voice.

You also discovered the meaning of structure, and how to construct your personal story.

Well done! Whatever you do with your writing from here, you will be moving forward – because you now know how to. You will most likely develop several of the pieces that you have already written; perhaps you will choose one particular element of your writing and develop it further. Whatever you do, I hope you feel inspired to continue along the writing path, and I hope you structure and write your book.

The Memoir Writing Workbook is now *your* personal memoir

journey. Read it often. Use it to write more of your thoughts. Share your memories with family and friends. Be proud of what you have achieved.

Writing takes thought, time and patience. Do not get discouraged; you have got this far and that in itself is a wonderful achievement. Give yourself deadlines to learn and improve your craft. Read your work to those that will help you. Read other people's memoirs. But most of all – keep on writing.

My deepest wish for you is that you continue to discover more of your self and your life journey through writing. I hope *The Memoir Writing Workbook* has inspired you to travel further into the magic land of words.

Keep Writing!